Unlikely Recruits

Unlikely Recruits

How God Enlists Horses to Help Veterans

Toni Mattson

Unlikely Recruits: How God Enlists Horses to Heal Veterans

© 2023 by Toni Mattson

Published by Green Pastures Press in association with Books & Such Literary Management. www.booksandsuch.com.

Unless otherwise noted:

Scripture quotations marked NIV are taken from the Holy Bible, New International Version®, NIV®. Copyright © 1973, 1978, 1984, 2011 by Biblica, Inc.™ Used by permission of Zondervan. All rights reserved worldwide. www.zondervan.com The "NIV" and "New International Version" are trademarks registered in the United States Patent and Trademark Office by Biblica, Inc.™

Scripture quotations marked (NLT) are taken from the Holy Bible, New Living Translation, copyright ©1996, 2004, 2015 by Tyndale House Foundation. Used by permission of Tyndale House Publishers, Carol Stream, Illinois 60188. All rights reserved.

Characters and events in this book are based on real people and situations but fictionalized with details and names changed to protect privacy.

All rights reserved. No part of this publication may be reproduced, stored in a retrieval system, or transmitted in any form or by any means—electronic, mechanical, photocopy, recording or any other—except for brief quotations in printed reviews without the written prior permission of the publisher.

Print ISBN: 979-8218232290

Printed in the United States of America

Dedication

This book is dedicated to hundreds, even thousands beginning with my parents, who through their brave military service inspired me to serve in my own way, by combining my love for horses and my deep respect and compassion to help veterans struggling with PTSD.

Unlikely Recruits is a culmination of years of work in the field of equine-assisted therapy. It is a tribute to the courage and resilience of our nation's veterans, and a testament to the transformative power of horses as healers and faith in action.

To the veterans we've been privileged to serve, the countless we still wait to serve, and to their families, I wrote this book for you. My prayer is that through these pages your voice is heard and you are better understood. Your guts and grit to push on, seek healing, rise above your challenges, and live your triumph stands as a powerful example for us all. Your willingness to trust me as you journeyed back to the light has been an honor of a lifetime.

Thank you and God bless you all.

WHAT PEOPLE ARE SAYING ABOUT UNLIKELY RECRUITS

"Hope. For veterans, caregivers, family members, and friends. There is hope. When the pain of lived experiences, especially those of veterans, is too great, horses and their human partners can provide the path to greater internal peace." Mary M. Kolar, Captain, U.S. Navy, Retired, former Secretary, Wisconsin Department of Veteran Affairs

"Within this book (*Unlikely Recruits*) you will learn of many stories like mine. A life I knew was over, no longer mattered. The concept of a horse helping me was something I could not fathom or begin to understand. The journey many of us have gone through leaves me in awe of the healing power of horses, which will show you a whole new side to their true beauty." Brandon M. Drost, Sergeant E5, U.S. Army Veteran, TEC Veteran Wellness Graduate

"This book is living proof that committed, caring people can still make a difference. Through horse and human interaction and bonding, veterans can relearn how to recognize their feelings, control their emotions, and come to trust themselves again - all valuable tools to help them succeed with their family, their work, and their relationships." COL David Church U.S. Army

"This book shares stories like mine which are sure to inspire many and spread the message of the healing power of Equine Assisted Psychotherapy." David M. Jeske, Sergeant, U.S. Marine Corp. Veteran, TEC Veteran Wellness Graduate

"INSIGHTFUL! A tasteful tribute to our vets and their needs! The nonverbal responses of the horses coupled with their wise human teams provide both a healing remedy for these vets, but also a sobering challenge for all to offer compassionate and courageous love, support, and understanding to these heroes who have sacrificed so very much for our wellbeing. A book that will keep you engaged from cover to cover." Dr. Lew Sterrett; Certified Youth, Marriage, and Family Counselor, President of Sermon On the Mount and Leaders by HEART, partnering with horses to win and train the next generation

"These stories are remarkable, heartfelt, so accessible, and do such a great job of sharing the magic, mystery, and healing power of horses. The faith-based summation and author notes add a valuable perspective and anchor the treasure of each story. Read it and be changed forever." John Murphy, Greatest Hits 98.1 Morning Personality, Midwest Family Radio

"(Unlikely Recruits) gives us all an invaluable front row seat to the amazing, transformative help, hope, and healing provided through horses." Mark Halvorson, News Director and Morning Show co-host for WWIB/WOGO, co-founder of Teamwork Africa, a nonprofit working in Liberia, West Africa

"As a veteran and veteran advocate, I was skeptical of Equine Assisted Therapy for veterans battling PTSD, brain traumas, physical handicaps, and moral injuries. However, each chapter of this book contains not only a true encounter but becomes a powerful acknowledgment of the special bond forged between a struggling veteran and a horse and what life-changing things can happen. This book is a must read for all." Jacob Leinenkugel, U.S. Marine Corp. Veteran

"The journey I experienced in Trinity's horse therapy changed my thought pattern for the rest of my life. I owe them my life. I would have drunk myself to death if I didn't receive their help. They gave me the tools to work through my daily life. I have a lot more good days now than bad days. I had never been around horses before my time at Trinity. I no longer am just surviving day by day, I am finally living my life. I will never be able to repay the debt I owe them. John C. Sarafin, E7, U.S. Army Veteran, TEC Veteran Wellness Graduate

"Trinity's horse therapy has changed my life. I knew from the first moment I walked the pasture that things were going to change. Week after week my confidence grew while my demons shrunk. The process is an uncommon one. It connects to the very foundation of your soul and helps rebuild you from the inside out." Nicolle A. Lillis, SPC E4, U.S. Army Veteran, TEC Veteran Wellness Graduate

As the daughter of a Vietnam veteran who wrestles with the traumatic effects of war, I could never understand the depth of his pain. Within the first chapter, Toni's breathtaking descriptions take you inside and close up to the courage it requires when our veterans with PTSD move through this incredible trust journey. It's a triumphant story of the hero and healer with hooves. With each step they take, your heart is simultaneously aching and expanding with gratitude and hope for the inner solace our veterans deserve." Sarah Stokes, Owner|Founder, The Juicy Good Life (business management consultant services)

"In *Unlikely Recruits*, Toni Mattson's wonderfully written accounts showcase the deep, meaningful horse-human connection and the healing power our equine friends are capable of providing for veterans and their families from all walks of life." Talya Purdon (horse rescuer and enthusiast)

ON ALERT...

The pages of this book are as real
as the experiences you have had.
Please know this book was written
with you in mind
and with the greatest of respect.
I ask you to be careful and kind
with your heart as you read it.

"The journey I experienced in Trinity's horse therapy changed my thought pattern for the rest of my life. I owe them my life. I would have drunk myself to death if I didn't receive their help. They gave me the tools to work through my daily life. I have a lot more good days now than bad days. I had never been around horses before my time at Trinity. I no longer am just surviving day by day, I am finally living my life. I will never be able to repay the debt I owe them. John C. Sarafin, E7, U.S. Army Veteran, TEC Veteran Wellness Graduate

"Trinity's horse therapy has changed my life. I knew from the first moment I walked the pasture that things were going to change. Week after week my confidence grew while my demons shrunk. The process is an uncommon one. It connects to the very foundation of your soul and helps rebuild you from the inside out." Nicolle A. Lillis, SPC E4, U.S. Army Veteran, TEC Veteran Wellness Graduate

As the daughter of a Vietnam veteran who wrestles with the traumatic effects of war, I could never understand the depth of his pain. Within the first chapter, Toni's breathtaking descriptions take you inside and close up to the courage it requires when our veterans with PTSD move through this incredible trust journey. It's a triumphant story of the hero and healer with hooves. With each step they take, your heart is simultaneously aching and expanding with gratitude and hope for the inner solace our veterans deserve." Sarah Stokes, Owner|Founder, The Juicy Good Life (business management consultant services)

"In *Unlikely Recruits*, Toni Mattson's wonderfully written accounts showcase the deep, meaningful horse-human connection and the healing power our equine friends are capable of providing for veterans and their families from all walks of life." Talya Purdon (horse rescuer and enthusiast)

On Alert...

The pages of this book are as real
as the experiences you have had.
Please know this book was written
with you in mind
and with the greatest of respect.
I ask you to be careful and kind
with your heart as you read it.

From the Heart of the Author:

For decades, I have been privileged to witness what some would call magic and others would call miracles in dusty paddocks and wood-lined arenas, in grassy pastures and steel-lined corrals.

The miracles happen when a troubled military veteran connects with a horse in our equine therapy program. The transformation from crippling PTSD, despair, and hopelessness to courage, determination, and hope used to surprise me. It no longer does. For whatever reason, God created something in the heart of a military veteran that resonates with the heart of a horse, especially a horse that fights its own demons.

Within these pages, you'll read the name- and detail-adjusted stories that are compilations of some of the very real and very desperate military men and women who have come to our equestrian therapy facility as what they thought was their final, agonized cry for help.

A horse answered.

God intervened.

And lives have been changed.

~ Toni Mattson, author and speaker,
equestrian therapy professional

Table of Contents

Chapter One: Today's the Day · · · · · · · · · · · · · · · · · · · 1
Chapter Two: Conquering the Godfather of Addictions · · · 10
Chapter Three: Mae Moments · · · · · · · · · · · · · · · · · · · 19
Chapter Four: A Gold Star She Never Wanted · · · · · · · 28
Chapter Five: Teens Tapping into the Heart of a Horse· 36
Chapter Six: Battle Buddy · 45
Chapter Seven: The Most Unorthodox Hug · · · · · · · · · 53
Chapter Eight: Crisis of Faith · · · · · · · · · · · · · · · · · · · 62
Chapter Nine : Obstacles That Free You · · · · · · · · · · · 70
Chapter Ten: Lie Detector · 78
Chapter Eleven: God's Amazing Grace · · · · · · · · · · · · 86
Chapter Twelve: Welcome To My Hell · · · · · · · · · · · · · 95
Chapter Thirteen: Living My Tornado · · · · · · · · · · · · · 103
Chapter Fourteen: At the Hands of the Potter · · · · · · · 112
Chapter Fifteen: Free Will · 121
Chapter Sixteen: Ribbons of Redemption · · · · · · · · · · 130
Chapter Seventeen: The War Called Grief · · · · · · · · · · 139
Chapter Eighteen: Better Than Before · · · · · · · · · · · · 148
Chapter Nineteen: You'd Do the Same · · · · · · · · · · · · 157
Chapter Twenty: Freedom Between Friends · · · · · · · · · 166

Acknowledgments · 177

Chapter One
Today's the Day

It wasn't the same as her other tearful requests. No more wishing, hoping, or waiting. It was a demand. "Either you get help, or we're done!" Call it self-preservation, self-defense, or whatever you like. It was today… or it was over.

Mia, the long-time, gutsy girlfriend of the veteran made the appointment. She entered first, greeted us first, sat first, and spoke first.

Aaron, a thirty-something Marine veteran, entered the assessment like it was an interrogation. His hoodie, ripped and faded, was pulled over his head, nearly covering his eyes. The vet made absolutely no eye contact and said nothing.

Mia knew him well. She'd lived with him for five fearful years, complete with his night terrors, insomnia, and drinking until blackout. But she confessed the one thing most frightening about him was watching his once bright blue eyes grow black and soulless.

The girlfriend thought she knew everything. But how could she? Did she know how many friends he lost in combat, or to suicide? Or how many "way-too-close" calls he barely survived? Did she know how desperately he wished his service pistol wouldn't have jammed that night in 2011? And how ashamed he was not having the guts to clear it and finish with a temple shot? She couldn't know because he never, ever let anyone near his internal bunker, not even her.

At the risk of oversimplifying my role, equine specialists are professional diggers and watchers. Trained to dig for hidden, seemingly unimportant details and watch how they help reveal our client's story.

But on this day, no training was needed to see the rage, anguish, and despair smothering Aaron. It was like a mangy, tattered blanket that reeked of decaying flesh. He despised it but wasn't willing to shed it. Not yet anyway.

It was obvious Aaron hated being at the equestrian center. His beet red face and pursed lips were so tight, I thought they'd bleed from the force. I watched the man's carotid artery pound, beat by beat, from across our six-foot table.

Breaking the uncomfortable silence, I explained, "Working with horses is different than most other therapies. We don't ask you to sit and talk about your feelings. In fact, we don't usually talk much at all."

It's hard to explain that the most meaningful conversation isn't heard, it's felt between the veteran and horse.

"It's about the relationship that grows between you and the horse, and what's picked up in the process."

Still not a peep. Not a sound except the *tick-tock, tick-tock* of the clock on the windowsill.

Trying to relieve the strangling silence, I asked, "So, do you have any questions? Do you think this is something you'd like to try? We could start this same time next Tuesday, if you'd like."

For the first time in nearly 90 minutes, Aaron raised his head, jerked forward in the chair, and looked the therapist and me square in the eyes. He slammed both hands on the table, leaned in, and let go.

"Well, I can tell you this, I'm never going to trust you two!" The flaming profanity that followed—aimed openly our way—could have scorched the table separating us.

Trying not to look shocked, I said, "Well, I guess that's something we need to work on, isn't it?"

He erupted.

What I'd meant to lighten the atmosphere, he took as a personal insult. He bolted from his chair and stormed out.

We peeked through the window as Aaron raced to his car and oddly paused before getting in. He opened his wallet and quickly glanced at a piece of paper, as if to be sure it was still there. He jumped in, and before the door closed fully, sped off, spitting gravel as he floored it.

His girlfriend Mia looked embarrassed and apologized for his outburst. She tried to explain through her tears, "He's tried every kind of therapy, but nothing helped. This was our last chance."

Walking Mia to her car, we noticed the tattered and stained sticker curling away from her bumper. It read – "I LOVE Veterans." She watched us read it. When our gazes met, her eyes flooded with tears. Sad and weary, she was barely hanging on. That was the last time we saw her.

We knew if we had half a chance, we could help Aaron. Nearly 90% of the veterans we serve say they're far better off having worked with our horses and our team.

The Trinity team is a powerhouse with horse, human, and Holy Spirit. This trio guides the "dance" between my therapist partner and me. Sometimes she leads from the head, sometimes I from the heart. No matter which, it was a worthwhile waltz.

Would Aaron show up a week later? We optimistically held the spot for him, but both of us agreed he wasn't coming. Imagine our shock when we saw his car speed in.

Torn between panic and praise, we spun like two tops on steroids, scrambling to grab our coats and phones. Before opening the office door, we paused to compose ourselves. I whispered to the therapist, "Let's not chat. Just a quick hello, then to the barn, and out with the horses."

For over a decade, I've walked down this cracked barn aisle. If concrete could talk... It might say how proud it is to sing the echoing *clip-clop* of the horse's hooves as they land on its floor. Or how it knows when a real horseman's "in the house" by watching them close their eyes and tip their heads back, intoxicated by the sweet, yet sharp aroma of the barn.

Or it might whisper how many confessions it's heard, and the torrents of tears that have fallen on its surface. Like us, the concrete might never want them to dry entirely, for fear the wounds and stories may be forgotten.

This really is a hallowed hallway. It touches my soul, and I hoped it would touch Aaron's as well.

Entering gate six, our gorgeous cream-colored draft took notice. Prince is neither shy, nor apologetic. He's an 1800-pound, full-blown, studded crown prince, who thinks the world revolves around him. For many of our vets, it does. He's possessive, protective, and playful. And if he picks you, you've hit the jackpot.

Aaron kept in step with us, head down, intently avoiding the "muffins" as if this were a dangerous Iraqi mine field. Finally glancing up, he stopped dead in his tracks, alarmed to see Prince on a straight path for him.

"Why is he coming this way?"

"To meet you," I said.

"Why?"

"Just to meet you."

Aaron suddenly seemed even more uncomfortable. He blurted, "I think I should've told you, I'm deathly afraid of horses!" After a spilt-second pause, he chuckled nervously. His levity was the first sign of his harsh outer shell softening.

Horses don't like discrepancies. They're remarkably sensitive and become troubled when our outside behavior fights our inside feelings. They're experts at reading the story our body language is eager to tell. That makes them perfect therapy partners.

Horses watch, listen, and evaluate every microscopic detail about us and their surroundings. Just like a combat soldier. If there's fear, they smell it. A shift in action, and they notice it. Something out of place, they sense it. Friend or foe. Safe or dangerous.

For a horse and a soldier, it's all about survival. Making the right call can mean life or death for both.

Aaron froze, paralyzed with fear. As the horse trotted up, he stopped only inches from Aaron's feet. The veteran's eyes were wide, his arms stiff and at his side.

Within a blink, Prince's massive head was softly pressing against the veteran's chest. Without moving his head, and speaking from the corner of his mouth like a rookie ventriloquist, Aaron squeaked out, "What does he want from me?"

"He wants to connect. Rub his neck. He likes that."

For nearly twenty minutes, we witnessed a love-fest as Aaron and Prince connected. Only days earlier, Aaron was aggressive and resentful. Only moments ago, fear-filled and frozen. Now, in *this* moment, he was loved. No fear, anger, or judgment. Just an uncomplicated heart-to-heart connection.

The session flew by. Now in silence, we retraced our steps back up the barn aisle. Seventeen stalls in all. But after we passed each one, Aaron walked more slowly.

As we reached the big double doors, we asked, "Will we see you next week?"

To our surprise, and like a friendly tornado, Aaron spun around, bear-hugged us, and said, "Yes. I can't let Prince down. I told him I'd be back."

Aaron returned the following week as promised, but he was "off." Touchy, sharp, and impatient. He scowled when he saw all we had mounded in the middle of the arena.

"Aaron, use anything you want from the pile to create something that shows us how you see your world today."

We stood back as he aggressively created pure chaos. He threw a handful of hulas across the arena, scattered cones and pool noodles everywhere. His creation was curving, winding, crisscrossing, and all leading to dead ends.

He stopped, then bolted to us, shouting, "There, I'm done!"

"Tell us about it."

That's all it took. Tears fell as he said, "This is my world. It's a mess. I'm a failure and a coward. I know what I need to do, but I don't have the guts to do it."

Without warning, the horse blew in like a typhoon and shamelessly upended his entire world, not leaving one element untouched.

Initially, Aaron was furious, but then relented, "Prince even knows how insane this is."

The therapy activity's second step was far more demanding.

"Now create something that shows us how you want your world to look." This would take hope, insight, setting goals, speaking his truth, and expressing his dreams.

"I want a life of peace," he said, suddenly subdued. "To feel like a man, and like I'm making a difference. To have the respect of my twin girls, to finish college, and marry the love of my life."

What a declaration! Honest and vulnerable. Brené Brown would be so proud. The emotional rubber was about to meet the road. That's when wall-building ends and hope and healing begin.

With one deep, slow breath, Aaron transformed before our eyes. Wiping any remaining tears, Aaron took the hulas and arranged them like Olympic rings. Tidy, symmetrical, and intentional. Then came the ground poles, like the spokes of a huge wheel, leading to upright cones at every end.

In moments, he turned to us, smiling from ear-to-ear. "This is it. This is what I want my world to look like."

As he began to explain, Prince began to circle. The horse watched the veteran's every move.

Aaron started with the rings, pointing to each. "The yellow one is my girls, Katie and Karlie. The red one is my career, the one I want. The green is my relationships, and the blue is Trinity Equestrian Center."

We wondered about the unidentified fifth ring. "Hey Aaron, how about the purple one?"

He paused, lowered his voice, and said, "That one's my faith. I'm wrestling with that, as it used to be the center of my life. And I miss it. I miss Him. But I hear how you two pray for me, how you talk to God like He's your friend, or Father. It seems so easy for you. I want that. So I'm still working on that one."

Prince finally stopped wheeling and took aim at Aaron's world, raising his hoof high and seemingly threatening destruction.

"Not again!" Aaron shouted.

The horse looked at the veteran as he landed his 12" dinner plate sized hoof squarely in the middle of one hula. Prince raised it slightly, slowly pulling it back and creating a wide, heavy groove in the sand. The horse raised it again, only this time, let it rest in the center.

Prince lowered his head, looked up at Aaron, and exhaled long and hard as if releasing every bit of stress, conflict, and despair Aaron had carried to that point.

"Look, he gave me his stamp of approval! Atta boy. Thanks!"

We closed our session with high-fives, celebrating the vet's progress. But like before, he quickly checked the paper in his wallet as he reached his car. What was that? Some affirmation, or a to-do list?

Aaron's transformation was stunning. Some say unbelievable, but we know better. We're blessed to have front row seats to the greatest restoration and redemption accounts ever.

For months, the veteran returned weekly, always thanking us for his Trinity visits. But our reward was seeing his incredible progress. His soft eyes and voice, the bounce in his step, how he now described himself. His enthusiasm, hopefulness, and leaning into his future were beyond our prayers. We thought finally the tattered blanket of torment was gone. Until his fifteenth week.

Aaron was on time, as usual, but with tears spilling down his cheeks.

"What's wrong? Are you okay? Are the girls okay?"

Gathering himself, he explained, "I've carried a suicide note in my wallet for more than ten years. It's always on me, just in case I decide today's the day."

My breath caught. It wasn't the first time I'd heard words like that. And they never rested easy on my heart.

"I decided today's the day alright," Aaron rolled on. "Not to take my life, but to declare I want to live. I WANT TO LIVE!" he proclaimed. "So, I burned it. How about that?"

We sat speechless, teary-eyed, and profusely thanking God.

The weeks of equine therapy had been devoted to praying, holding space for Aaron to rediscover his faith and believe he was worthy of his own healing.

For Aaron, it was fifteen grueling weeks of challenges, leading to epiphanies and transformations. Fifteen weeks of renewing his relationship with God and embracing forgiveness and grace.

And in those fifteen weeks, Aaron experienced a divine deluge of change that redefined who he was, his relationships—human and Holy—and his future.

Father, thank You for the privilege of leading Your divine and transformational work at Trinity and beyond. Thank You for the connection between You, Prince, and Aaron, and how his life is forever changed and blessed because of it.

Author Note

Suicide among our veteran population continues to steal twenty-two lives a day. Good, honorable, creative, courageous people who have served our country—gone.

For them, there was no hope or healing, only the demons that chased them to the end of their wits. Stuck straddling the past and present, war and peace, and the inconceivable notion of surviving combat only to succumb to life at home.

Those who've made the trade of all trades. The ones who traded their own safety to stand in the way of bullets, bombs, and brigades so they could protect us. They traded our slumber-filled nights for their horror-filled ones. They traded their peace of mind for high anxiety, flashbacks, nightmares, and the tauntings and terrors of PTSD that cause them to exchange life for death.

Do you know a veteran who struggles like this? Do you notice shifts in behavior, appearance, or language? Pay attention and speak up with love and support. They need to feel safe, seen, heard, and respected.

Sometimes all that takes is a few words of encouragement or recognition like, "It seems like a tough day for you. What can I do to help?" "I don't know what you've gone through, or what you're going through, but I do know that I'll be here for you no matter what."

Do you struggle? Does Aaron's story sound painfully familiar? If so, please know help is out there. It's accessible, confidential, and like the therapy at Trinity, free. No matter what city or state you're in, equine centers are there to help. If you're having a hard time finding someone who offers Equine Assisted Therapy, we'll help you find one. And if you need it, the national Suicide Hotline is 988. It's a 24-7/365 support line.

Chapter Two
Conquering the Godfather
of Addictions

"They prescribed nine different medications to numb my pain. Nine!" the veteran barked. "Are they trying to kill me?"

Lying in a ditch for hours after an AK-47 round shattered his left ankle, Marco's dream of retiring with the "full load" of military benefits was shattered too.

Surgeons did their best, but sometimes things get so torn up, it seems impossible to find all the pieces to reassemble them.

"I was no good to them — probably never would be again. So with a handshake and a medical discharge, I was shipped stateside," Marco said, wincing as he shifted his weight.

The Pain Rating Scale stops short of the level that would log this veteran's pain. It was white-knuckle intense on his good days and totally unmanageable on most others.

They called it pain management. The veteran called it government-sponsored addiction.

"I've seen it thirty, forty times. The Godfather's my favorite movie, and it was playing in the background." Marco smiled, his eyes only slits. "It was the scene where the *family* gathered for a meeting of the minds. They inventoried the room to check attendance. Just like me inventorying my pills."

My therapy partner and I could only guess where this analogy was going.

Marco straightened his invisible lapels and put on his best Sicilian accent.

"I have the *codone* brothers — hydro and oxy; the "*anti*" triplets — anti-depressant, anti-convulsive, and anti-inflammatory; my *made* cousins — demerol, trazodone, and morphine. And, of course, the Godfather himself — Fentanyl."

Some of the veterans we work with are only with us for a short time. Their issues are identified and dealt with well and quickly.

Then there are the more complex cases, like Marco. He had the trifecta — a problem with pain, pills, and purpose.

PTSD is a battle of the mind. Even a well-adjusted twenty-plus-year-old soldier grapples with all they see and do in a combat zone.

But a seventeen-year-old male enlistee can't possibly sort out all he's witnessed because he doesn't have that degree of brain power yet.

It's not a criticism — it's human biology and psychology.

I love knowing *why* we do what we do. And in Marco's case — I blame the PFC.

No, not a Private First Class — his PreFrontal Cortex.

This part of our brain has the mountain-sized task of managing our reasoning, problem-solving, comprehension, impulse control, and more.

But the PFC doesn't fully develop in young men until they're around twenty-five-years-old. Expecting our seventeen- and eighteen-year-old male servicemen to manage the unpredictable circumstances they're routinely exposed to is asking them to draw on critical skills they won't fully possess for another seven or eight years.

Marco was in that predicament.

It's a long-standing therapeutic fact – you can't make progress if you don't feel safe. Feeling heard, cared for, and respected is why our veterans trust our program.

"Every assessment I've had made me feel like a caged animal. The shrinks asked loaded questions, then sat back while they picked apart my answers," Marco said.

"Not here," I said, hoping to put his mind at ease. "Our process is about building connections. There are not a lot of questions. We let the communication come from the activities and encounters you have with your horse."

Knowing Marco was medicated almost 24/7, I needed to keep him safe during our herd walk and sessions.

We started in the mini pasture. Full disclosure, the only thing miniature about this herd is their size. Their attitude, stamina, speed, and curiosity are all far beyond most of our full-size horses.

I flanked Marco as we walked from one horse to another.

The therapist and I could tell none of the minis were interested. It's impossible to miss when they are. Nose in the face, muzzle in the pocket, and following like a puppy are all signs the horse wants to connect.

In the private turnout to the south was an injured mare. She was on pasture rest, pain medication, and a strong anti-inflammatory.

"What's her deal?" the veteran asked. "She's worse off than me. Look at her eyes."

"Reina injured her fetlock joint during a squabble in the pasture. That joint is like our ankle," I explained, wondering if the vet caught the parallel. "She's pretty medicated, so her eyes show it."

"I'll take her," Marco said in a snap. "If there's one horse on the ranch that knows what I'm going through, it's this one."

Even though my therapy partner and I had a different treatment plan in mind for this vet, we'd learned long ago to yield to the Spirit.

"Are you sure, Marco? This encounter will be very different than what you could have with other horses."

"Nope, I'm good with her," Marco said. "What will we be doing for her?"

"Well, a horse with her restrictions has a daily regimen of meds, standing stretches, lower leg massage, and rewrapping the joint," I said, detailing the task and expectations. "We need to see some progress — not perfection. She may never be 100% again."

"That's like what my physical therapy regimen was for my ankle," the vet clarified. "Go figure. We both have ankle issues."

BINGO.

"Can I start with her next week?" Marco asked.

"Your safety comes first. The treatment this mare needs will take being really close to her back feet, the area of her injury, and you may need to move fast," I explained, trying not to sound discouraging. "We'll review everything next week and go from there."

When Marco walked in the following week, we instantly saw a difference in his demeanor. He seemed more alert and focused.

"Good morning, Marco. Don't you look chipper today," I said.

"No kidding, you look different. Are you okay?"

"Yeah, I actually feel really good. If I'm gonna be around Reina's rear-end, I wanted my head on straight, so I lightened my meds," Marco said.

"You can take only what you think you need?"

"Yeah. Each day is different anyway." The veteran smiled. "But today is special, so I wanted to be at my best."

The therapist, Marco, and I pulled up a seat and reviewed the horse's treatment protocol. Everything was laid out on the table. Vet wrap, round-edged shears, liniment, a dish of applesauce, pills, crusher, and broad nose syringe. If Marco was going to help with Reina's care, he needed to know the *what* and *why*.

"Before you ask anything from her, you need to give her something," I explained.

The care this mare needed would require her to trust him.

"What you'll give her is a favor. Find something you can do for her that she can't do for herself. Find a spot she can't reach and give it a good scratch. Do it until the look of enjoyment leaves her face."

Overdoing a good thing isn't a good thing.

"See if I got this straight," the vet began. "I give before I get, trust allows treatment, and we're aiming for progress, not perfection, right?"

"That's it. Let's get at it."

The vet was the first to enter the turnout and followed my coaching to the letter.

"Hey girl, what kind of a day are you having?" the vet asked. "No one ever asks me that. I struggle with the pain in my ankle every day."

Marco scratched between Reina's ears. Reina's lips loosened. "Does that feel good, girl?"

We watched as Marco warmed up to the horse and slowly increased his request for trust.

He carefully removed her leg wrap, examined the wound, and reported what he saw. "It's pink but not red. No drainage, but still raised at the suture line. There's a bit of proud flesh on both sides, but not enough to be concerned."

"How do you know what a healing wound should look like and what *proud* flesh is?" I said as I glanced at the therapist, then back to the vet.

"Didn't I tell you I was a field medic in Iraq? You'd be surprised what I saw and know how to assess."

No wonder the veteran looked so comfortable with the medical pack.

"Here's the part that's over my pay grade, though. I need to do the leg stretches, but I'm a little concerned she doesn't trust me enough yet." Marco stood with one hand resting on the horse's rear and the other on his own hip. "How can I tell if she's ready for this?"

"If you have a *big ask* at the rear end, you start by asking permission at the front end." I said as a hint. "Her eyes will tell you if she's ready. Let her know what you need to do and check her eyes. Soft and relaxed? You're good. Alert and wide? She needs more time."

Both my therapy partner and I stood far enough behind him not to obstruct his assessment.

"I don't think she's ready, do you?" the veteran said, disappointed. "Her eyes look wide and wary."

Despite Marco's skill, the mare wasn't ready for him yet.

I finished each treatment step with Marco right next to me. I couldn't help but think he'd make a great veterinary assistant.

Marco was one step ahead of me the entire way. Handing me the shears, vet wrap, and crushing and mixing the meds before I asked.

I could tell being an Army medic was a great source of pride for him. But after his injury and the long list of drugs he was taking, the likelihood of being accepted into an EMT program was slim.

What a shame. He had everything he needed to do well and too much of what would hold him back.

Time moved forward, but Reina wasn't improving as fast as we had hoped, so we called our local veterinarian in to see what changes we needed to make.

Not realizing it, we set up an overlap of appointments between Marco's next session and Doc's visit.

I explained to Marco why Doc was coming and asked Marco's permission to tell the veterinarian he was in our program and tasked as Reina's caregiver.

Marco agreed instantly.

The veteran held Reina's lead rope while Doc began his exam.

"So Marco, you're this mare's caregiver, right?" Doc asked without looking at the vet. "Give me an update on what's been happening with her and why there's no progress."

The vet began giving a treatment summary on the spot.

"Her meds have been given as scheduled, the lower leg's been wrapped and relieved two times a day as you've instructed," the veteran reported as if he was Doc's assistant. "The manual stretching and bending has been difficult. Reina's not fond of that and resists. Sometimes she all-out refuses."

"Well son, seems you've got a good understanding of what's happening and what's not." Doc nodded. "What's your background?"

"An Iraq medic. But I took an AK round in my ankle that blew it to bits. There wasn't much left, so the VA prescribed a boatload of pain meds and gave me a medical discharge," Marco said, his tone tight. "I'm in the middle of trying to dig my way out of that hole."

"Good for you," Doc said. "You'll do it. Don't give up. Don't ever give up."

My therapy partner shot me an inquisitive look.

"You're good at this — really good. Best of all, you still have a chance to write your story. You choose how this chapter ends," Doc said. He wiped his nose. "My son wasn't as lucky. He was a medic in Afghanistan, got injured bad like you, but he couldn't get ahead of the addiction. It took him."

No wonder Doc seemed so eager to encourage Marco. It was personal.

"My son was supposed to come back and help me with my practice," Doc said as he struggled to get up from ground level.

Marco quickly handed the lead rope to my partner. "Let me help you. I can do all that bending and squatting. It's good for me to stretch my foot and leg out," the vet said.

Doc straightened, looked at me with a raised eyebrow, and asked Marco, "You're not looking for work, are you?"

Marco had been honest about his struggle with pain meds and the Doc was offering him a job?

"I applied to the EMT certification program but got put on hold," Marco said. "Got the brains and experience for it, but I need more space between me and my habit for them to accept me."

Doc asked, "Okay Marco, what does this mare need to get some progress going?"

The veteran looked like a student called on in class but he hadn't read the assignment.

"Um... seems she needs to move. The injured area needs to be loosened up, or it may never regain its proper motion," Marco said as he gained steam. "If she won't tolerate manual stretches, we could try short walks. If she tolerates that, we walk, and we walk. Short trips that slowly grow to longer ones. We intersperse cold water therapy in between to keep the swelling down."

Doc stood back, rubbed his forehead, and squinted.

"We don't let her get too dependent on the pain meds," Marco said. "We start slowly, backing her off now but keeping up the anti-inflammatory and water therapy to give her the relief she'll need." Marco looked up at Doc.

Both the therapist and I were thoroughly impressed by Marco's understanding of what this mare needed, and what she didn't.

"How far off am I, Doc?" the veteran asked. "I'm just thinking of what would've worked better for me instead of drowning my system with narcotics."

Doc leaned against the fence post and said, "You hit it on the nose, son. On the nose."

Marco softly scratched Reina's forehead and asked, "Well girl, should we try a short walk?"

Some may say this isn't equine-assisted therapy. I beg to differ.

Finding therapeutic solutions with the assistance of a horse is what we know works.

I admit, most often, the work we do with our veterans is more straightforward. They come with predictable issues caused by specific experiences.

But how the horses help can be far less predictable.

It often is with horse-led activities, allowing metaphors to develop and help clarify the veteran's strengths and struggles. Or tapping into the *biofeedback* capabilities of the horse that respond to and reflect our emotions.

Or it can be much less structured and far more life-led.

Just like it was for Marco.

This veteran's therapeutic journey didn't begin in an arena filled with hula hoops, ground poles, and instructions to build "your world."

This time the healing began when Marco met Reina and realized they both struggled with a similar future-altering injury.

Both horse and human — in their own way—were on parallel paths of how the temptations of the mind and body were leading to a conversion of the heart and soul. The deep desire to heal and become someone — something — new was why they would do whatever it took to live the life God created them for.

Even though Marco was eventually cleared to start his EMT program, he happily chose to stay on as Doc's assistant.

I think it was Doc's way of honoring the son he lost. He became a loving and devoted mentor to help Marco step into his glory and purpose.

The veteran continued working with us and Reina until the mare passed all benchmarks asked of her.

It was quite a sight to see — Marco and Reina enjoying their walk down Trinity's driveway. The veteran with his pronounced left leg limp and Reina with her right rear roll.

They made the perfect team.

It was never about perfection — only progress.

Father, thank You for being the one who defines the work we do with Your precious servant — the horse. You allow the beloved relationship to change everyone within its reach. All become healed and all are living the life You created us for.

Author Note

It's our job, and the job of every equine therapy center, to provide a safe, peace-filled, and enriching environment. We do this for our clients, team, volunteers, and horses by upholding the highest standards and best practices in our industry.

All of Trinity's team members eagerly maintain continuing education, clinical supervision, appropriate certifications, memberships, and training. All of our Mental Health providers are Wisconsin licensed Therapists.

To learn more about Equine-Assisted Therapy and the worldwide organizations Trinity is certified through, visit EAGALA.com and PATHinternational.com.

CHAPTER THREE
MAE MOMENTS

It was like a vintage pinball machine. Flashing lights, blaring sounds, targets, bumpers, and ramps. It was nanosecond fast and impossible to predict. This was Andrew's brain.

His years in the military taught him to treasure his laser-sharp sense of awareness. Exquisitely trained, Andrew gathered and sorted countless fragments of intel, instantly classifying them as distraction or danger. The barrage of sights, sounds, smells, and sensations would bury most. But for Andrew, the evaluation was never late, never wrong, and never forgotten. It was physically and emotionally draining.

The veteran came to us a frustrated and angry college student after eight years in the Army.

"I don't get it! Why was I okay in Iraq where hostiles threatened us every day, but I come unglued in a classroom? I'll flunk out if you can't help me."

"Help you do what?" we asked.

"Take the stupid test, like everyone else." Andrew's voice and hands shook. His pale pink face turned fire-engine red as he continued.

"I couldn't stand it. It was so loud! First it was just background noise, but then it exploded into a contest of which one would drown out the other—the girl pounding her foot under her desk, the professor gnashing his gum, or my number two pencil grinding into the paper, tearing it as I blackened my answers. It was making me crazy."

It's called hypervigilance. Textbooks say it's "a state of extreme alertness causing confusion and sensory overload."

But a soldier would say it goes way deeper. It routinely triggers brutal memories that raise holy havoc on their judgment, making it nearly impossible to distinguish past from present, or reality from delusion. Sadly, the five senses assigned to protect Andrew now commit treason by tricking his psyche into thinking he's back in Bagdad, Kabul, or Kandahar.

Andrew confessed how he handled his recent college exam environment. "I screamed, 'EVERYONE SHUT UP!' I tried explaining to my professor it was too loud for me to concentrate. That I was a vet with PTSD and can't turn off the noise in my head. I pleaded for him to just let me take the test alone in a quiet room."

Instead of compassion, Andrew received condemnation.

In a mocking voice, Andrew recounted the professor's reaction. "There will be no preferential treatment for anyone in my class. No one. No reason. Now sit down, take the test, or fail."

Andrew had never felt failure. Only success, promotions, and citations. *Oorah!*

PTSD is often caused in an instant, but can linger for a lifetime. It rears its monstrous head without warning or waiver. Andrew needed to understand what he was dealing with and what to do about it. He needed to meet Mae.

Hiking deep into gate one, we found her in the farthest corner. Mae, our most recently rescued mare, seemed quiet and kind. That's why I was so infuriated. Most horse people consider being a horse's caregiver a high calling. A privilege. Some even see it as a spiritual responsibility. Not this horse's previous owner.

An anonymous caller was frantic. "Please, you've got to save this horse! The owner said if no one takes her today, the horse is dead."

We hung up the phone, hooked up the trailer, and in a flash were speeding down the highway. But to where? The scant directions were hollered between the caller's plea for help. Thankfully she pressed redial, giving us the address, along with a stiff warning. She whispered, as if someone might hear her. "Just be careful. They say the owner's a crazy one, if ya get me. She's done this before."

We pulled up to the arena and hopped out. The massive arena door was standing open, so we stepped in. I announced to the three girls huddled up, "We're from Trinity, and we heard there's a horse here who needs a new home."

The barn owner stepped out of the shadows and walked towards us, sporting an artificial smile and arrogant swagger.

"Who told you that?" she asked sharply.

"Oh, you know the horse world, if there's a pony in trouble everyone knows about it," I casually said.

We knew the woman's reputation with the County Humane Society, from the many visits and warnings we heard about. She snapped back, "There's no horse in trouble here."

We surveyed the dimly lit ring, barely able to glimpse the horse tied at the far rail. As we got closer, we could see she must have once been strong and spirited. But that spirit surrendered years ago to this woman's overriding, underfeeding, and relentless corrections.

The woman mounted up, drove the spurs deep into Mae's sides, painfully pushing the horse to show her long extended trot, and tight turns. We knew the production was only to distract us from the horse's condition and level of pain.

But nothing could disguise it. What she had done to this horse's body would require daily supplements and routine injections to have any chance of managing the damage. But what she did to the horse's mind and spirit should be considered criminal.

The woman began her third round of walk, trot, canter when I shouted, "No need to go on. We've seen enough."

She hollered back while drilling her barbs even deeper into Mae's sides, "It looks like she's trying, but she's not. This horse gave up years ago. She's gotten lazy and defiant, and I won't carry her anymore! Everyone here pulls their weight, or they're gone."

This time I wasn't nearly as friendly. "Stop pushing that horse and bring her here."

Mae's owner pulled up with a hard stop, jumped off, nearly jerking the bit from the horse's mouth, while yelling at her for dropping her lead.

My partner snatched the reins from the owner's hands, and declared, "We're done here. There'll be no more abuse for this horse."

Spitting and sputtering as she chased us to our trailer, the woman tried to convince us it wasn't abuse we saw, just her version of training.

"So killing her is the answer?" I snapped back, confirming her plan.

The owner barked, "That's what you do when they quit trying. When they're no longer useful."

I stopped, turned slowly, and looked her square in the eyes. I paced my answer so she wouldn't miss a word. "No ma'am. That might be what you do, but that certainly isn't what we do." I hollered to our team, "Let's load her up. This horse isn't dying today."

As I opened the trailer door, Mae broke from our grip, and leaped in with so much force she broke the front manger. Horses are smart. They have an inside track on emotions, energy, and intentions. She knew the favor we were doing her, and we knew she'd return it.

As I jumped into the truck, I pulled one single dollar bill from my pocket, rolled down my window and handed it to the owner saying, "Here, now you've even been paid for her."

Once arriving at Trinity, Mae was less than enthusiastic about her long walk through our unfamiliar barn. Shadows bouncing, hooves echoing, and the soft snapping of the electric fencer startled her to a full stop countless times, making this trip nearly as long as the one to get her here.

All night long, her sad cries calling out to her lost pasture mates kept me awake. No one returned the call. It broke my heart.

Days passed without Mae taking but a few steps. We knew her condition needed slow and calm movements, but just standing would only aggravate it.

"So I'm going to learn about horses huh? That'll fix me?" Andrew nervously asked as we walked toward Mae that day.

"Horse therapy is more about learning what makes you tick, rather than learning about the horse itself," I replied. "Working with them helps us help you. It's all about what you learn from the relationship that grows between the two of you. Don't worry if that doesn't make sense. It will."

Gate one sits at the farthest edge of our property. It borders two state highways made popular by semi drivers for the short-cut it gives to the city's south side. Two fields over, cradled high in the pines, rest two sandbox-sized eagle's nests. The high-pitched screeches, blasting Jake brakes, and honks from friendly motorists are commonplace on any given day. It was the perfect place to start for someone who considered sound their enemy, and silence golden.

We broke our own rule. Normally, we let the horse pick the veteran, or vice versa, but not this time. We knew it had to be Mae and Andrew. They both had soft hearts, with heads that refused to let them forget.

As we approached, the horse stood without moving a muscle. Was it to avoid the pain of walking, or did she welcome the encounter? I knew her eyes would tell me everything I needed to know. Mae's were wide, but not wild.

Andrew was understandably nervous when we asked him to move closer to the horse. He preferred his horsepower tucked under the hood of his 1967, candy-apple red Mustang.

"Just stand there for a moment while Mae accepts your presence," I said. "When you feel comfortable, move to the other side, and do the same."

Horses have two sides to their brain. Each independent, like two different horses. So what you do on one side, you need to do on the other. It keeps them balanced and at ease.

I knew a connection needed to happen between the two before anything meaningful would take place. But week after week it looked like no progress was being made. That all changed in week seven.

Mae surprised Andrew with a queen's welcome. The horse took two full steps towards him, gracefully bowed her head, and slowly raised it up. That was the day when Mae's eyes told us her heart was open and ready.

Then it began. We asked Andrew to slowly place the palms of his hands on the horse's side and let them rest there. Mae was noticeably confused by the gentle contact. She was trained to respond immediately to any pressure on her sides or suffer the former owner's sharp consequences. She lifted her head high and gave it a good whip to notify us of her unrest.

Andrew tried again, only this time speaking to the horse in a slow, sweet tone.

"I'm not going to hurt you. We're in this together. We're a lot alike, you and me. Both afraid of sounds that surprise us or that remind us of bad things. Right? I want to help you, and I think you want to help me."

Many overlook what's communicated by a simple touch. It's thanks to the network of micro-circuits that run through our bodies which allow us to experience and respond to sensations. This system works the same for horses, but in a much more profound way.

Their entire body is as sensitive as our fingertips. It's how a horse feels the tiniest mosquito land on one single hair. But it's the touch of a human that seeps deep into their soul, revealing our intentions. It's our touch that tells them if we're friend or foe, trustworthy or not. It's our touch that tells them whether we want a partner, or just a tool to be discarded when they're no longer useful.

And it's our touch that tells them our story.

Andrew's kind contact told Mae who he was, what he wanted from her, and what he wanted for her. When you allow the horse to come face-to-face with your light and darkness, the healing begins.

The veteran gradually moved his hands across the landscape of the horse's rib cage, feeling scars and scabs left behind by the previous owner's sharp riding spurs. He passionately apologized to her for them, as he paused over each.

Mae closed her eyes as if to internalize the forgiveness and freedom Andrew delivered. It was an act of grace that freed them both. Releasing them from anger, fear, and judgment. It was then that Mae finally seemed to value the visits as much as Andrew.

My therapy partner and I knew we'd hit paydirt when the veteran agreed to close his eyes while laying hands on the horse. For someone who relies on all his senses to keep him safe, this was a cataclysmic leap of faith. For nearly thirty minutes Andrew stood without even shifting his weight.

He followed our request to the letter. "Close your eyes and take a big cleansing breath. Inhale through your nose, exhale slowly through your mouth. Envision the breath you're drawing in as a holy healing, a godly light moving through your fingers, and penetrating deep into Mae's heart. Now, receive that healing light back from her to complete God's work. Your Father wants to heal you both. You as His son, and Mae as His servant."

Andrew was completely engrossed, entirely absorbed in the moment, and intensely connected to Mae. He slowly opened his eyes, sliding his hands down to his side, saying "That was amazing! I only felt my heart beating in sync with Mae's, and my breath matching hers. It was so quiet and calm."

It was a true divine delivery. Andrew stopped the clamoring in his mind by focusing on only what he chose to let in. He simply shut out the rest. It was the grounding he needed.

When Andrew returned to school, his first stop was his professor's office to apologize. The veteran assured him he was ready to take the test, like everyone else.

He grabbed the exam, took his seat, and closed his eyes. Andrew took a deep cleansing breath, planted both feet flat on the floor, and remembered his moments with Mae in the pasture. He picked up his number two pencil and wrote an A+ test.

Weeks later, he stopped by the ranch for a surprise visit with his dear friend Mae, and of course to brag to us about his final grade.

Rescuing Mae was an act of kindness, and a spiritual exchange. We didn't need her fancy moves, we needed her fearless heart. We didn't need her grand performances, we needed her grace-filled spirit. And that's just exactly what God gave us. When we rescued the horse, God rescued the veteran. What a perfect partnership.

Jesus, thank You for the amazing healing You provide through Your kind equine servants. Help us become better and better at tuning out all the distractions of this world, so we are diligent about listening to You, and for You. Thank You for being our rescuer and redeemer.

Author Note
5 STEPS TO MANAGING YOUR HYPERVIGILANCE:
(You'll need a tablet or journal and a pen)

1. Understand what hypervigilance is.
2. Recognize your triggers.
3. Identify your reactions to each.
4. Choose your method of grounding/calming for each.
5. Journal it.

LET'S BREAK IT DOWN
What is Hypervigilance? Hypervigilance is the elevated state of constantly assessing potential threats around you, and is often the result of trauma. It's a state of high-alert, always tense and 'on guard,' and always looking for hidden dangers, both real and presumed. It's stressful and exhausting to maintain, and...it's manageable, even treatable.

What are *your* triggers? Since hypervigilance is a very personal condition, the key to controlling it is to be aware of *your* triggers. Knowing your triggers helps you prepare your response to them. How do you do that?

Pay attention to what causes you to become anxious or feel unsafe, and write it down. Some situations and events you already know will trigger you, like the 4th of July sights and sounds, a crowded elevator, or traveling under an overpass. Others will take you by surprise like loud unexpected noises, someone coming up behind you, finding yourself in an unfamiliar situation. But what are *yours*? Make a list.

Know how you react to your trigger. In your journal, write down how you've reacted to each trigger in the past. Be thorough and honest. You're the only one who's going to see this. Then, next to that, note how you'd *like* to react to this trigger going forward.

Ideas for grounding and calming. You now have a list of your triggers, how you've historically reacted, and how you *want* to react in the future. It's time to find ways that'll help you get or stay grounded after you've been triggered.

There are lots of methods to get grounded, and to calm yourself. Here are a few. Take a break, take a walk, get away from the triggering environment. Take deep breaths – slowly inhale through your nose, hold for a beat, and then slowly exhale through your mouth with pursed lips. Count to 10 or 20 very slowly as you take deep breaths. Put your favorite music on, go for a walk or exercise. Movement helps your physical and mental health. Use calming essential oils.

Journal it. Writing down your steps to manage your hypervigilance makes them more powerful, and doable. When you see them, one-by-one, picture the path that will lead you to your progress. Tracking your victories and your stumbles will help you see shifts you need to make so you can experience more progress. Your journal will become your story of not just managing your hypervigilance, but how you conquered it. This process takes practice and a bit of devotion. But, practice makes progress.

You can do this!

Chapter Four
A Gold Star She Never Wanted

On June 4, 1928, twenty-five mothers led by Mrs. George Seibold met in Washington DC to establish the national organization American Gold Star Mothers, Inc.

Mrs. Seibold had lost her son, 1st Lt. George Vaughn Seibold, a WWI Battle Aviator, during an air fight on August 26, 1917.

When I was a kindergartener, the prospect of being award a gold star motivated me to learn to tie my shoes the fastest, put my crayons away on time, and tuck my nap matt nicely in its place without being told. Then, I had no idea what a gold star could really represent.

Mrs. Constance Engelhart lost her daughter, US Army Specialist E-4, Patricia A. Paulsen, during an ambush in Kandahar on March 14, 2014.

That was the date Connie became a Gold Star Mother. That was the day she was awarded a gold star she never wanted.

"The success of our organization continues because of the bond of mutual love, sympathy, and support of the many loyal, capable, and patriotic mothers who while sharing their grief and their pride, have channeled their time, efforts, and gifts to lessening the pain of others.

We stand tall and proud by honoring our children, assisting our veterans, supporting, and healing with each other."
— an excerpt from the historic American Gold Star Mothers, Inc.

Connie was one of five Gold Star Mothers who visited Trinity Equestrian Center in the fall of 2015.

"We asked to come to Trinity because this is the place where many of our veterans came for help. Whether they were sons or daughters, they needed hope and healing. This place provided it," Mrs. Englehart explained.

"We are honored — truly honored to have you here," I said, as I embraced each mother. "I'm sorry for your loss, and want to thank you for your sacrifice and the unconscionable *trade* your family made to protect our way of life and our country."

These mothers came to learn how we help veterans.

They were desperate to meet a horse who carried God's light on its back, piercing the darkness that threatened to drag tortured souls into the black abyss of suicide.

We were eager to meet their needs.

When we entered the arena, our chairs were already arranged in a sweeping circle. Wide enough for our horses to mingle among the mothers safely, yet close enough for the ladies to feel connected.

The mothers called it the *honor hour*. One hour set aside to share the stories and honor their lost loved ones.

Connie started. She told how her only daughter, Patti, insisted on following her brothers into the Army, even though she hadn't the stomach for either conflict or killing.

As they continued sharing, the horses continued socializing. They meandered in and out, between and behind the ladies, stopping when something piqued their curiosity, or to console a sorrow-filled mom.

Buddy was the friendliest horse. Gunner the most sensitive, and Reina was the *horse version* of Florence Nightingale — the mother of all nursing.

These horses were the perfect fit for what these mothers needed.

Pauline, the newest woman to the group, gathered her emotions, promised not to cry, then detailed the day she was notified her son, Ethan, had been killed. "Two uniformed military men knocked at my door and asked if I was Mrs. Pauline C. Conrad. I said I was. They asked if I was the mother of Corporal Matthew P. Conrad. I said I was." She covered her mouth with her hand, struggling to go on.

All of us gathered there knew where the story was headed. The sight of two military personnel at the door was enough to tell the tale.

"Ma'am we are so very sorry to inform you that your son, Corporal Matthew P. Conrad, was killed in action on four, September, 2019. He was part of a forward unit that took heavy fire..."

Her voice trailed off.

Matthew's mom squeezed her eyes tightly to stop tears from falling. Between her gasps for air, she repeated, "I'm sorry, I'm sorry."

Gunner was consumed by Pauline's pain. The gelding stood post at her immediate right, as if he was her Honor Guard. He broke form to rest his muzzle on her arm. The horse deliberately amplified his breathing and slowed its pace to model what the mom needed to recompose herself.

The Gold Star Mother then unknowingly matched the horse's breathing. When she opened her eyes, Gunner's tender brown eyes softly meet hers. The gelding looked as if he were weeping too.

The mother stroked the horse's face to thank him for his kindness.

Horses are incredibly emotional animals. Some express it more than others.

Gunner is known for his willingness to take on the sadness and weight of the therapeutic encounter. The horse *holds* the human's trauma so they can experience freedom from the sorrow — if only for a few moments. This pause is what encourages the veterans to hold on, to move on, and grab on to healing with both hands.

Whether it's a veteran who is haunted by their demons, or a mother who is haunted by her loss, the need for healing is absolute.

This deep soul work is often as difficult for our horse partners as it is for our human partners. It's impossible for our horses to consult a teammate and be reminded to take a break. That it's time to be cleansed and calmed by good self-care.

That's our responsibility as caretakers at Trinity. We are in charge of our horse's self-care. We take them out and free-graze them. We give them their favorite dish — grass or grain, while we massage them from nose to tail.

We take them out on a nature-filled trail to help clear their hearts and senses.

It's our job to make sure they have abundant time to simply be a horse. Not a therapist, not our partners, and not healers — just a horse.

Reina, our Florence, knew what our clients needed. This mare sensed deep festering wounds and knew what would soothe the sting.

While two more moms took turns detailing the happy and heartbreaking memories of their lost sons, Reina sashayed between and around them in what looked like a deliberate pattern.

The others sat wide-eyed and curious until one mom finally asked, "Is this horse making a figure eight around these ladies? Isn't that the symbol of infinity?"

"It could look like that," I said, leaving it open to interpretation. "What do the rest of you think?"

"Looks like it to me," Connie remarked. "But what does it mean?"

"Who knows what infinity symbol represents in traditional faith circles?" I asked.

They exchanged glances and shrugged shoulders, until one mom broke the silence. She was the only mother who had not made any comments yet. "Doesn't it mean regeneration and resurrection — a new beginning?"

Reina stopped making her pattern and stood in the center of the chairs.

The mare didn't move.

"It means to be without limits," the mother finished.

If the footing in the arena had not been of sand and dirt, you most definitely could have heard a pin drop.

The two circled mothers stood and embraced, taking turns holding each other up.

One asked, "What do you think it means? What the horse did? What does it mean, Toni?"

"In our work, the things that happen during a session always draw different conclusions from different veterans. It depends on their history, their struggles, and where they are in their healing process. However, what I will say is that horses are remarkably intuitive. They often know what we need and how to deliver it. I believe that's how God helps them help us," I said. "It's not hocus pocus — it's Divine. And in Divine terms, infinity means immortality."

The space became very quiet as the mothers seemed to evaluate all they had seen and felt today, and what it might mean to them.

The serenity came to a sudden stop when Buddy, *Mr. Friendly*, barged into the circle. He's our goofy gelding, but the perfect horse to provide a bit of comic relief to close our time.

He made his way to each of the mothers, personally greeting them by flashing his big flared nostrils in their faces. He wasn't being aggressive, just a bit *extra*. That's his style.

The ladies politely chuckled.

Then, out of the blue, one mom broke out in a full-belly, I-can't-stop-laughing jag. She let out a huge snort. "That horse's big nose reminds me of when my son snuck up behind me and..."

Another mom chimed in. "That's hilarious. My daughter did the same thing once, and I laughed until..."

The ladies layered story upon story, not waiting for any to be finished before starting the next.

"One time my son surprised us by..."

"Have your kids ever..."

Slapping their legs, hooting as they threw their heads back, and unapologetically spilling the beans on every crazy, zany, and even embarrassing thing their kids ever did, they continued.

This is what Buddy brings out in people — the healing power of laughter.

When we inhale oxygen-rich air, it charges up our heart and lungs, flooding our brain with endorphins and dopamine. It crushes cortisol, the stress hormone.

If we live in a constant state of stress, anxiety, even sorrow and grief, our bodies rebel. They blast our blood pressure and heart rate sky-high, tighten every muscle we have, and shut down our digestive system.

Laughter is good and needed medicine, just like the Bible says in Proverbs 17:22.

The *honor hour* rolled into a two-and-a-half-hour honor-athon.

It was exactly what these mothers needed.

These Gold Star Mothers learned and laughed, cried and comforted each other.

They experienced why the work we do does what it does. Why we choose horses as our partners, and how God moves mountains to get His message across.

Our Father meets us precisely where we are. He knows what our heart and soul need to heal and move forward.

He knows — because He made our heart. He formed our soul.

I walked the moms to their cars, not saying a word. Why compete with the euphoria dancing in the air and the deep sense that something very special, very life-changing happened there that day.

Before we said our final goodbyes, Connie said, "Toni, the moms want to know, when we first arrived, you thanked us for our sacrifice and the trade our families made. What did you mean by a trade?"

"The reason I used the word *trade* is because of what we were taught by the hundreds of veterans we've worked with. We've spent thousands of hours in session with them, in a mutual process of listening, asking questions, and learning from each other."

I paused to make sure the ladies could hear me.

"Many veterans who come to Trinity for help say the expression "Thank you for your service" feels almost hollow and meaningless to them. That those words feel like a knee-jerk reaction, only blurted out when someone learns they're a veteran."

What I was saying could be perceived as disrespectful, so I tried my best to be sensitive.

"They told us the word *service* didn't adequately describe what was given up. The veterans insisted the contract was better expressed as a trade. I would say — a *sacred trade.*"

I sat on the edge of our picnic table, and continued, "Your sons and daughters traded their safety, security, and even their sanity for ours. They traded days, months, even years of distorted and dangerous flashbacks for our peace of mind."

My heart was racing and my voice was rising.

"They traded their freedom for ours. We have the privilege of living the life we choose. They live the life their military experience created for them."

I stopped and looked at each of the mothers.

"And in a split second — with no hesitation — your sons and daughters traded their life for ours."

It is a trade more Christ-like than I've ever known.

Father, You are without limits and without boundaries. You offered the ultimate trade. You refresh us, refill us, and flood us with the hope and healing only You can provide.

Thank you, Jesus. Amen.

Author Note

My mother, Faith M. (Brahmer) Schmidt, was a WWII US Army nurse serving in Europe. She saw firsthand what war did to those fighting it.

Mom dealt with lost limbs, lost hope, and lost lives.

Whether a past war, or one not yet waged, the loss and pain never changes.

Faith and her team of servant souls did their best to patch up our American soldiers in hopes they would survive the trip back to a US military hospital. For them to heal, or to go *home.*

She completed her commission in a Texas military hospital.

When discharged, Mom continued nursing and became the supervisor of surgery at a Central Wisconsin regional hospital for fifty-plus more years.

Faith Mary Schmidt died at the age of 94 and was buried with full military honors.

She was remembered for the "Florence-like" encouragement she gave every person in *her* operating room before they went under the anesthetic — and under the scalpel.

Mother would say, "I'm with you now. I'll be with you through your entire experience, and I'll be with you when you wake up. I will not leave you."

Reassurance every patient needed to hear.

Reassurance from Jesus every Christ-follower holds dear: "I am with you. I will be with you through your entire life. When your time here draws to an end, I will be with you to take you home. I will not leave you."

Colors of the Stars and what they represent:
Gold Star Mother – has lost a child in the service of our country.
Silver Star Mother – mother of a son or daughter who has been wounded in action.
Blue Star Mother – mother or stepmother who has a son or daughter who is serving, or who has been honorably discharged.
Red Star Mother – mother of a captured or missing service member.
White Star Mother – mother who lost a son or daughter service member to suicide.

Chapter Five
Teens Tapping into the Heart of a Horse

Communication equals connection. How we define communication matters. And how your teens define it seems ever-changing.

Do they text, use memes, gifs, disappearing Snapchat, hush-hush abbreviations, and friend-to-friend codes?

Has the art of talking become one of the many casualties in the evolution of our language? Instead of using it for inclusion and deepening understanding, it seems like it's used as an exclusionary tactic. Like our long-ago treehouse clubs. If you know the password—you get in.

Trinity not only provides free equine assisted therapy to veterans, but we also extend that service to their children.

Whether six, sixteen, or twenty-six, family life can be brutal for those with either deployed parents or ones struggling with military experiences.

Logan was a high school Junior. He was good at science and math, but great at making baskets and scoring touchdowns. Rumor had it, he was up for a full-ride athletic scholarship and more than ready to escape the chaos in his home.

His father was a two-time deployed Marine veteran with PTSD and his mother was on her third send-off in the US Navy.

In the evenings, Logan hid in his lower-level bedroom until his father finished a case of beer or a bottle of booze. The chances of avoiding a combative conversation were better that way.

Logan's best buddy lived next door with his father – a school counselor.

Mr. C, as Logan called him, saw all the signs of an at-risk young man who needed support and structure. He recognized this teen was riding a razor thin rail that teetered between confidence and fear, calm and agitation, and enthusiasm and sadness. Maybe even depression.

In a whirlwind of contrast, another teen we served at Trinity, Venus, was a fashion-forward high school freshman who dreamed of one day being a New York City clothing designer.

Her father served "more tours than he needed to" according to the teenager and her mother. This bubbling resentment deteriorated the once friendly family ecosystem and eroded any remaining shred of civil communication.

Both Logan and Venus, along with many other students over the years, participated in Mr. C's off-campus adventures.

Visiting the library to get a card; serving meals at the homeless shelter; seeing a production at the community theater; visiting the Boys and Girls Club; doing a mock interview at Jobs-R-Us; taking a tour of the County Jail; and closing with Trinity's four-week equine assisted attitude adjustment after-school camp.

Mr. C's goal was to expand his student's thinking. To expand their perception of themselves, their abilities, and those of others. To expand their opinions and assumptions beyond their personal prejudices. And to expand their empathy and respect for people regardless of their status or present situation.

This school counselor's purpose in life was to grow his students' understanding of how their choices produce predictable consequences—good and bad. And how authentic communication, grace, and forgiveness can play monumental roles in their lives — if they allow it.

I love working with Mr. C's groups. When these kids get it, they're never the same again.

Horses have their own way of communicating.

My dog wags her tail when she's happy, barks when she wants out, and licks to show me affection. People smile and laugh when they agree or find something funny. They grumble and gasp if they're displeased or frightened.

But horses are harder to read. They require more visceral ways of communicating.

When you learn their language, you'll understand what exquisite communicators they are.

Logan walked from Mr. C's car with Venus a few steps behind. He came in a jersey from the college he hoped to play for and tattered flip-flops on his feet. Venus was decked out in knee-high heeled boots and a bedazzled crop top.

Mr. C introduced Logan and Venus. "Both have deployed or veteran parents."

"Thanks for your sacrifices," I said with all sincerity.

"Why thank us?" Venus snapped. "We're not the ones who leave our families and make everything ten times worse!"

"No, you're not. But trust me, I know how tough it is for those left at home."

Mr. C shot me a sly wink, but I already knew where to take this.

"Often it's the kids who are stuck holding the bag, and sometimes even holding their parents," I explained. "What your mom or dad go through can be barbaric. And what you go through while they're gone, and even when they return, can be as rough."

The teens looked at each other and shared a "teen-code" facial expression.

I had no idea what it meant.

We started in the barn, stopping at every stall so Venus could evaluate if the horse's names on their doors matched their looks.

"Venus, you put a lot of importance on looks, don't you? What about me? Be honest, I can take it," I prodded.

The young lady was merciless. "You look like you're in your late forties, early fifties with that hair. You obviously don't care what impression you make because you're wearing dirty boots, worn-out jeans, and a flannel shirt from the seventies."

Logan cut her off, "Venus, why don't you just tell her how you really feel. You're being rude! Knock it off."

"It's okay Logan. She's right—to a certain degree. I only care what my horses think about me. And what I think about me."

Her nose curled up as if she'd sucked on a lemon.

"I'm the one who needs to respect me at the end of the day. It has nothing to do with how I look or what I wear — it's what I feel in my heart."

I knew my response was about to turn into a sermon, but I was on a roll.

"Sure, when I clean up, you'd probably never recognize me. But my work, what I stand for, what we do here – that's what matters. How I connect and communicate with God, my horses, and the people in my life matters."

I was hoping there'd be a crack in their armor for my message to seep in.

"If I get dirt on my boots, maybe even manure on my jeans, that tells me I've made a difference today. I might have righted a wrong, saved a horse, or had fun with my grands."

I motioned to Mr. C that the end was near.

"So what may disgust you delights me. And hopefully there will be a time in your life when you'll be able to tell the difference between a job and a calling. Trust me, that's when you'll start making a difference."

Standing in the pasture, I handed each a lead rope, a halter, and instructed them to pick a horse and bring it to me.

Once they realized I wasn't kidding, Logan aimed for the closest horse, while Venus went for the prettiest one.

The athlete saw himself as an achiever, but ignored what his overgrowing ego was communicating to the horse. He charged up to our normally congenial gelding, but the football star was too busy looking cool to notice the halter was upside down and he was about to shove the chin buckle into the horse's eye.

"I usually say there's no right or wrong way to put this on, but how you have it, Logan, might be pushing it," I said.

Venus was on her third attempt to halter the shiny horse in the pasture.

Neither of them asked for help. They chose to bumble instead of be humbled.

Horses are huge and powerful animals and not always cooperative. Even a cocky teen is out of their league when they're up against the size and strength of a horse.

They're smart and remarkably sensitive. Though we might have trouble reading horses' feelings, rest assured they have no trouble reading ours and are eager to set us straight.

"It's a dance," I said. "With an animal this big, it's all about the *give* and *take*. Leading and following while you discover the delicate and delicious balance between the horse and human."

I could tell they were listening, but trying hard not to look like it.

"With a horse, it's not about what you get from them, but rather what you give them and get in return. There's a huge difference."

Putting a halter on a horse seems like it should be easy, but it's actually harder than you think. It demands awareness—both of oneself and the horse. It requires the student to put aside their fears and put on their humility.

When they can do this, true self-confidence explodes.

"Looks like you both got the halters on. Good work," I said, not commenting on how oddly they hung on the horses. "Make a few laps in the arena and we'll call it a day."

"Aren't we going to do something with them? Like a ride?" Venus asked sharply.

"You are most definitely doing something," I remarked. "This is how you start connecting and learning to communicate with each other. You may think you speak a different language, but you'll find you really don't."

I decided to postpone my sermon on how being shoulder-to-shoulder with your horse launches the relationship, etc. I knew it'd be wasted at this point.

"When you come next week, you need to wear flat-heeled boots and clothes you don't mind getting a little dirty," I said.

Logan kept quiet while Venus let loose. "There's no way I'm wearing that to school. I'd rather die than have my friends see me like that."

"It's up to you. But if you don't come dressed properly, you'll be sitting out. And lose the dangly earrings. You're not impressing anyone here and I don't want them accidentally jerked out. This is all for your safety... and the horse's."

The following week Logan came with the prescribed attire while Venus went cross-grain.

"Good job on your clothes, Logan. Venus, how about you? Where are your ranch clothes?"

"I told you I wouldn't dress like that."

"You did say that. But what I say isn't a suggestion. You'll sit out today. Let's go Logan, your horse is waiting for you," I said, motioning for Venus to sit in the chair outside the round pen.

"Walk your horse around the pen a few times, then we'll meet in the middle," I said.

Logan and George made three laps and squared off.

"Now, drop your lead rope to the ground and ask George to stay while you walk away from him."

George ground ties better than most on the ranch. His willingness to stand still as you make circles around him is an outcome of time well spent. Time spent cultivating a relationship, spent learning each other's language, and spent asking instead of telling.

None of that happened—so no ground tying would either.

"How do I get him to do it?" Logan had asked the million-dollar question. "You said I have to talk to him and get him to listen to me, right?"

"Just grab him and make the horse stand," Venus barked from the sidelines. "If you jerk hard enough on that rope, he'll stand still!"

"Nope." I stopped her. "If you had the right clothes on, I'd invite you into this process. But you don't—so I won't."

"But I wanna come in," she whined.

"Next week, if you come prepared."

Logan spent the rest of the session talking, walking, petting, brushing, and getting to know George's love language.

Surprise, surprise. Venus chose to follow the rules the next week.

"There, I wore what you said I had to, so no laughing," she said, rolling her eyes.

"You mean because you look like me now?" I replied, with an oversized grin.

Because what we're doing in these sessions with teens is called equine-assisted *learning*, no therapist is involved. It's teaming with the horse to learn social and life skills.

How to get along and solve the conflicts if you don't.

As I helped Venus figure out the fine art of horse and human connections and communication, Logan conquered the art of ground tying.

"Logan, well done! How does that feel?"

"It feels amazing," Logan said, patting George's neck. "He could've walked away, but he chose not to. He's a good boy. A really good boy."

When it was Venus' turn, the spicy teen started by ranting to Dallas how stupid she felt, dressed like that. With every failed attempt, Venus got more frustrated and the horse grew more belligerent.

"How am I supposed to do this if she keeps stomping away from me?"

"Did you give your mare a reason to stay?" I fired off. "Have you tried to become her friend? Talk to her or treat her with respect?"

After the fifth attempt, I thought the horse needed a break and the human needed a lesson.

"We're gonna try something different. Unclip the lead, put that long orange stick in your right hand. Extend your left arm out, pointing to a spot in space ahead of the horse's nose," I said.

I calmly reminded her the stick is an extension of her arm — not a weapon.

"Focus your energy on the horse's flank and use the stick to encourage your horse to move where your left hand is pointing."

"She won't move!" Venus whined. "She's not listening."

I saw Logan resting against the rail on the other side. He was watching intently.

"Horses don't respond to whining, Venus. They respond to clear communication," I explained. "Dallas needs to know what you expect from her. Start again."

This is another exercise that looks easier than it is.

"That's it. Focus on her flank using the stick to direct your energy and encourage her with your voice to move forward."

They got it.

"Now drop the stick and use only your body."

Venus nodded, matching the beat of the mare's gait.

"Do you feel it? Do you feel the magic of being in harmony with your horse?" I asked. "This is what happens when you and your horse work as one. Now bring her down to a trot, Venus, then a walk, and when she stops and looks at you — turn and walk away from her... slowly. See what she does."

"What's she doing? I don't want to turn around to see."

"Dallas is following you," I said, smiling. "Now stop, slowly turn toward her and let the mare walk up to you."

Venus couldn't have done better.

"Tell your horse what she needs to hear from you," I said, softening my voice. "What do you want her to know?"

Venus opened up. "You're so beautiful. I mean inside and out. I can't describe how I feel. I've never felt this before. You are so true to yourself."

The teen was teetering on tears. "I want to be as comfortable being me as you are being you. Will you teach me?"

The former fashionista couldn't hold it anymore. She sobbed as she stood next to Dallas, covered in horsehair and her horse's slobber. "Thank you for being my friend — my only real friend."

We spent the remaining weeks perfecting the craft of creating an authentic relationship and the resilient *give* and *take* of it.

The tension of the two tightly wound teens was now released. They learned all that Mr. C had hoped. And from the horses, they learned life's *dance*—the beautiful two-step of connecting and communicating.

Venus began reciting, "When you work with a horse, it's not about what you get from them, but rather what you give them and get in return. Isn't that right, Mrs. M.?"

I was flattered. It was the first time she called me that.

Logan piped up, "It's the same for people, parents, and friends too, right?"

"Indeed," I agreed.

As they got ready to be picked up, I laughed, and asked, "Hey Venus, you gonna change clothes or go back to school like that?"

"I'm going just like this. This is who I am. I'm not hiding behind some fake bedazzled life anymore. Dallas taught me to be me. She taught me that I am enough, just as I am."

"You sure are. You both are," I said, giving a good-bye hug.

I love working with Mr. C's groups. When these kids get it, they're never the same again.

Ever.

Father, thank You for making Your lessons unmistakable. You are the Great Teacher. All patient, all knowing, all forgiving, and all loving. Thank You, sweet Jesus. Amen.

Author Note

Learning the nuances of how horses communicate with us can be fascinating. There are many resources to dive into if you want more on this subject.
- thehorses.com
- parelli.com
- equinehelper.com
- animalcognition.org
- *From the Horse's Point of View* by Debbie Steglic
- *Horse Speak* by Sharon Wilsie
- *The Equine Listenology* by Elaine Heney

Chapter Six
Battle Buddy

"I can't sleep. Can't eat. And I sure can't forget. They said it'd get better, but it's not," growled Duncan, a 43-year-old, four-time deployed Army veteran.

"Every night I'm back in the sandbox, on patrol with Karl." Karl was his only boyhood buddy and best man at his wedding. "He demanded to take the lead that night." Duncan buried his face in his hands and continued.

"Karl stopped, turned to me and whispered, 'Did you hear that?' and BOOM, there was an ear-splitting blast, and he was gone." Duncan's voice cracked and trailed off.

"I don't just mean dead, I mean, his body was gone." He revved up, "I should've died, not him! It was my turn to go first. I killed him!"

Survivor's guilt mixed with haunting nightmares serves up a dangerous cocktail. Their recurrences torment countless combat veterans, making them easy targets to seek amnesia from pills or alcohol.

"I can't live like this anymore," Duncan insisted. "It's been four years and every single night it repeats, like a broken record. This isn't living."

Veterans, like many others, don't understand how a horse can help humans. How a hairy four-legger can become a friend that helps tame their demons. That was Duncan.

"Can't tell you why I'm here." He exhaled. "I heard you have horses that help vets somehow. No offense, seems like a stretch, but worth one last try."

My therapy partner at the Equestrian Center shot me a subtle but alarmed glance. One last try? Was he contemplating suicide?

We know every tour of duty is vastly different. Every deployment, more than just a pin on the map. Every experience produces memories, pleasant or traumatic. Every memory lives in our psyche, adding to our life's story.

Sounds harmless enough, right? Sure, until the painful and distressing memories, the horrifying and humiliating ones refuse to retreat quietly. Not when they demand to be relived, over and over again.

We're often told things so unsettling, it takes days to shake their shadow. In a session nearly ten years ago, one of our veterans described his "dark passenger." Before saying a word, he backed against the arena rail, as if for leverage. He took a two-fisted death grip on some unseen object, then began.

"It's like dragging my dead, decaying corpse with me everywhere I go. So heavy, I wanna drop it. But I can't—it's me. But that person died in the desert sand long ago. My honor, morality, my decency—all dead. The hope that I'd be like I was before—dead too. Will God forgive me? Never! Fallen comrade? No. More like the walking dead. That's why suicide is so tempting. It ends this hell I'm living."

Trinity Equestrian Center sits on 67 acres with miles of Kentucky-like white fences. As you drive in, you know this place is special. You can feel it. In fact, shortly after we bought it, an old prayer warrior friend of Rev. Billy Graham visited Trinity. She stepped out of her car, took a wide stance, outstretched her arms, and proclaimed, "This is holy ground we're standing on folks. Holy Ground!"

That stuck with me.

Over our more than twenty years, we've partnered with our horses to help hundreds of struggling veterans find hope and healing. This uncommon, yet globally practiced process starts with a connection between the horse and veteran that commonly happens during something we call a *herd walk*.

This special walk winds us through each pasture, giving the veteran a chance to trudge alongside the horses. It allows them to meet each one, make a connection, with the goal of creating a relationship with one. It's this relationship that will keep the veteran coming back each week. This walk is the first step in breaking down barriers, and launches the healing process.

"Let's start in that pasture." Duncan said as he pointed to gate two, the only pasture with no horses in sight.

I wondered what made him choose this pasture over the others where horses were waiting at the gate? Did he think no horses meant no discussion? Or did he figure the long walk to find them would give plenty of time to talk?

Clearly it was the "long walk, lots of talk" scenario, because Duncan exploded in a flurry of chatter, but oddly, only about Karl. Where he lived. Where they met. His range scores, special training, plans when he got out. On and on, but nothing about himself.

Finally, we spied the herd. Stopping nearly fifty feet from them, we had Duncan take a deep breath, watch them, and tell us what he saw.

Duncan piped up sadly, "That polka dot one looks lonely."

We asked, "What makes you say that?"

"None of the other horses are near him. He feels alone, pushed out from his unit. Abandoned."

Everyone has a story they struggle with. Time with the horses helps veterans reveal it, and process it in the moment. What they share helps paint the picture of the war between their head and heart.

We pay attention to every detail. That's how we help them make sense of their history, and reconcile it. We help them make peace with their past, so they feel safe living in the present, and leaning into their future.

"Which horse do you want to get to know?"

Instantly Duncan replied, "The dotted one. What's his name?"

"If he was yours, what would you name him?"

The veteran stood there, not moving or talking. We thought maybe he missed the question, or refused to play along. Finally, he answered,

"I'd call him Buddy, like my battle buddy. You know, just like Karl. I'll call him BB." Duncan never asked the horse's name again.

It was an uneventful first encounter until Joey, a sassy buckskin pal wanted in on the attention. When Joey stepped closer to Duncan, BB spun around at lightning speed to intercept him. Pinning his ears, BB let out a startling squeal, and planted himself between the veteran and Joey, cocking a rear hoof. No one was going to cross this line, not even a friend of ten years.

Instead of being startled, Duncan smiled and blurted, "Was he protecting me? It looked like he was ready to go to battle for me. To kick that other horse's bootie! Just like Karl. He was always stepping in and standing up for me. Would BB do that too?"

I softly answered, "Looks like he would."

Duncan turned away to wipe his tears.

The horse knew his work. He knew it would take time to help Duncan accept the loss of Karl. He knew he had to help seam together Duncan's tattered heart through the relationship they would build. BB knew he needed to guide Duncan across the bridge from hopelessness to a fresh start. From grief to acceptance. And ultimately, from guilt to appreciation that he was still alive. No small task.

Wasting no time, BB came from behind, placed his head squarely between the vet's shoulder blades, and launched him forward. Nearly falling to his knees, Duncan righted himself, swung around, raised his fists, and barked, "Don't you push me! I'll lay you out!"

Not being intimidated, the horse walked right back up to Duncan, slowly lowering his head. Now eye-to-eye, BB exhaled the longest sigh I've ever heard from a horse. It wasn't in anger, or some weird horsey challenge. It was as if BB understood the only way Duncan was going to survive was to keep moving forward. The horse was being the battle buddy Duncan needed. You know, "never leave a fallen comrade."

Push after push, BB moved the stubborn veteran across the pasture. Finally, Duncan relented, turned, and hollered, "OKAY, OKAY. I GET IT. YOU WIN!" Softening his tone, he continued, "You want me to move on, is that it? Isn't that why you keep pushing me?"

BB let out a friendly and forgiving whinny.

"Did you make him do that? You trained him to do that, right?" Duncan asked.

I chuckled, "If we could do that, we'd be making crazy big bucks on some Hollywood set."

It's important our veterans know we don't train our horses to respond in any particular way. When we join them in their pasture, we've entered "their world." They're free to stay or walk away. To act, react, and behave exactly how they feel. That's what makes our work so honest and reliable.

Duncan was devoted to his time with BB, never missing a session, and always accepting our challenges. Except when it came to unearthing the lie, the root of the guilt and shame that held him captive.

I've never met a horse that didn't love grain. At Trinity, they get it, but only occasionally, and will do nearly anything for it. They'll walk over perilous ice, enter a tight, dark trailer, and even sacrifice freedom for capture. Grain is irresistible, and the best tool for us to "poke the bear."

It was our eleventh week when we decided it was time for the game Keep Out. Our instructions were straight-forward. "Use what you can reach in the arena to create a barrier. A bunker that you will keep your horse out of."

Duncan quickly complied, creating roughly a 15-foot circle made of pool noodles. He looked proud and content even when we led BB in the arena and removed his halter.

"Starting now, keep your horse out of your bunker. Do whatever it takes to keep him out."

Duncan rolled his eyes, as if to say, "This is child's play," while he successfully kept the horse out. BB casually turned to re-enter from the other side, but Duncan calmly stopped him saying, "Nope, you can't come in here."

We upped the ante by placing an empty grain pan in the middle of his bunker, and re-issued the instructions. "Keep your horse out."

BB surprised Duncan by bolting over the pool noodles, dashing in for a quick peek in the pan. The horse was intoxicated by the residual sweet aroma of the grain's molasses. You could see the frustration in BB's eyes when he realized the pan was empty.

Duncan sensed a change in the horse's attitude, but managed to redirect him by saying, "Get out! Keep out!" Duncan became noticeably more defensive, now realizing this would be harder than he thought.

Raising the stakes one final time, we added a full scoop of the irresistible treat. Our instructions couldn't have been more grave. "Keep your horse out of your bunker, or he will die!" Game on – for us both.

Dust and noodles went flying as BB pursued the bunker, as if it was his last meal.

We hollered, "Can you keep BB out? No matter how determined he is? No matter how hard you try? Can you keep him out?"

Our version of Keep Out isn't the game we played when we were knee-high. This one is intense, frustrating, and always revealing. We needed Duncan to understand that his attempt to keep a twelve-hundred-pound animal away from his coveted grain was as impossible as it was to keep his adrenaline-addicted Army buddy from ignoring all obvious signs of danger and darting to his death.

Duncan pushed on BB's chest, shouting and swearing at the top of his lungs. Duncan ultimately threw his body in front of the horse, attempting to stop him, and "save his life," but nothing stopped BB. The horse pushed right by Duncan.

Gritting his teeth, physically and emotionally exhausted, Duncan spun around and landed on his bottom in the dirt. He finally realized no matter how hard he tried, he couldn't "save" BB.

Struggling for air, he mumbled, "I couldn't stop him, not when he got in that mood. No matter what, he'd never listen to me when he was like that."

"When who got like that, Duncan? Who's the horse?" we pushed.

"It's Karl! It's Karl. He wouldn't listen to me!" he barked.

We allowed Duncan to catch his breath, then pursued, "What do you mean when he got in *that* mood? When he got like *that?*"

Duncan bounced to his knees and shouted, "He'd get this weird, crazy look on his face and demanded that he go first, instead of taking turns like we were ordered to. It's like he had a death wish. The fear fed him—like an animal."

There it was. The lie Duncan believed for years was revealed, and blew up right before his eyes. The truth was, Karl's addiction to the adrenaline blasting through his blood stream caused him to do dangerous, unpredictable, and irresponsible things that ultimately led to his death. Duncan didn't cause it, and could've stopped it.

Duncan spent twenty-three weeks with us. Working with BB was cathartic for him. His nightmares subsided, until having one was a blue-moon event. He proudly admitted BB changed his life, and that survival sometimes comes down to simply putting one foot in front of the other, over and over. And he admitted, some of the best teachers in life don't need to speak to teach.

Father, thank You for being our Battle Buddy. We all need to be reminded there's a divine upside to every grizzly downside, if we allow the grace of God to shine into the darkness. Thank You for being our redemption story!

Author Note
Things to Know about Survivor's Guilt
- Survivor's Guilt is defined as feeling guilty for surviving something when others didn't.
- Symptoms related to this condition are: obsessing over your actions during the event, mood swings and angry outbursts, feelings of helplessness, desire to isolate, trouble sleeping, and thoughts of suicide.
- 90% of people who survived an event when others died report experiencing symptoms.
- Many people who struggle with Survivors Guilt wonder; "What could I have done to keep this from happening? "Why didn't I stay with them?" "It should've been me." "I should've been able to prevent this."

- Be honest about how you feel. Feel it, share it, and believe that it's a normal reaction to what you've experienced.
- Boost your mood by doing something meaningful for others, maybe volunteering somewhere to make a difference.

Chapter Seven
The Most Unorthodox Hug

Her eyes were merely one set of ninety watching through the broad wooden rails of the round pen. Nothing about her stood out...except those eyes.

It wasn't their color or eagerness to watch the demonstration or to make new connections and friendships similar to what I saw in the other ladies' eyes.

It was what I didn't see that drew me to them, that drew me to her.

Trinity Equestrian Center has been the host of the Wisconsin Women's Veteran Retreat for eight years. We love sharing our "home" with this group of veterans who eagerly, some desperately, come to have their cups filled with peace, inspiration, and renewal. To have their mind, body, and spirit expanded by the hope that new possibilities provide.

They come in need and leave inspired.

From all across our state, they pour in, hoping this day, on this ranch, with these horses and these fellow female comrades and devoted providers, will change them.

Most guests come in friend pairs. She didn't. She was alone. Not only in the physical sense, but I suspect, in every sense.

We kicked off the day with a demonstration of "how to" in the round pen. How to connect with a horse. How to convert that connection into a relationship, and ultimately how to transform it into trust. This process is the very foundation of our work. Without it, we'd go nowhere.

"Connecting comes naturally for both horse and human. We're both creatures that thrive when we're in a community, among friends, and living our purpose. However, the potency of a horse's sensitivity and intuition puts humans to shame," my teammate began.

"Did you know a horse can feel your heart beating from as far as five feet away? And within those sixty inches, your heart rate tells them if you're anxious or apathetic, flighty or grounded. Their ability to tap into your energy and emotions is what reveals your intentions. But it's when your body comes in contact with theirs that the translation of your story begins."

I tag-teamed in, "They interpret and internalize our energy. Positive or negative, friend or foe, they sort it to gauge if you're trustworthy or not. But it's our touch that either wins their heart or causes it to wane."

Some think describing this process as we do is a bit *woo-woo*. But in our world, it's the very fiber that weaves the fabric and creates the tapestry's pattern, which discloses the veteran's story and struggle. Like Joseph's coat — the technicolor one. It shows the many memories of growth and grief, hurt and healing, and desires and disappointments. Wearing it is both frightening and a badge of courage.

The loner walked from one break-out session to the next, not staying more than a moment at any. Stretching, mindfulness, soul care, massage, the joy of journaling. It was a plethora of experiences to engage all five senses — maybe even the sixth.

Our retreat is a one-plus day event starting the evening before around the campfire. The woody aroma, the orchestra of crackling sounds, and dancing red, orange, and white flames are the perfect backdrop.

The night before, I'd greeted the women around the fire with "Welcome to Trinity, ladies! We're thrilled to have you here again and look forward to our time together. This is your opportunity to relax and be renewed, and it's our time and honor to ensure that happens.

Tonight is all about fellowship. Catching up with those you've met from years past and building new friendships."

The loner had been there, but I'm not sure why. She sat far from the fire, head hanging so low it was as if her thoughts were so heavy she couldn't manage to hold it up.

I sat in the open chair next to her and began, "Hi, I'm Toni, one of Trinity's founders. I'm so glad you're here. What's your name?"

"Samantha, but most people call me Sam," she said with only one quick glance up.

"Is this event new to you, or have you been here before?"

"No, I usually don't do things like this. I'm pretty shy, but something made me come."

"Well, I'm sure glad you're here. Trinity's a place where everyone can feel safe and cared for. Enjoy yourself, okay?"

She nodded as I got up to greet other guests.

This event had eleven strategic activities, therapies, and experiences for the nearly one hundred female vets in attendance to sample.

It was designed to be a "come as you are and do as you please" gathering. It's our way of supporting not only the Wisconsin Department of Veteran Affairs but also the devoted women veterans who've served our country and were changed because of it.

I kept my eye on Sam, staying open to more encounters if the Spirit so moved.

Sure enough, the next day, I saw her leaning against the front gate where a herd of horses played. Some of the older horses were napping. It looked like the Midwest version of the series "Heartland."

Sam was glued to the horse with the Rapunzel-like hair and inquisitive nature.

The mare had many talents. We partnered with her in our riding and non-riding programs, even the one designed to serve those struggling with Alzheimer's and memory loss.

But most of all, this horse was remarkable at creating connections.

I stood from afar, enjoying the look on Sam's face — calm, dreamy, and very content.

The timing was perfect. The horse needed her medication, so I thought an invitation for Sam to help might open her up.

I approached her in plain sight, not wanting to risk startling her.

"Hey, Sam, I see you've noticed our most flamboyant mare. She's beautiful, isn't she?"

"She looks magical," the veteran remarked.

"She needs her meds. Any chance you'd like to help me?"

"No," she quickly said. "I love horses but haven't ever been close to one. I fell in love with them as a child, in my mind and heart, but never in 'person.'"

"I can change that, if you want. This mare's calm and quiet."

"What's wrong with her?" Sam asked.

"She has asthma. When she gets excited or anxious, she starts breathing hard and pacing. She had it when we got her, but now it's bad enough that she needs treatment for it."

"I know what that's like. I have asthma too. What's her name?" Sam inquired.

"If she was yours, what would you name her?" I asked.

I knew the question was more therapeutic-like than she might tolerate, but I thought I'd give it a whirl since it seemed like the Spirit created a therapeutic moment.

"Bella!" she blurted out, almost without time to think.

"I think that fits her perfectly. Are you sure you won't help?" I nudged.

Clearly, the answer was no, as she turned and walked away without answering me or even saying goodbye.

Maybe she took my request as pushy or as asking too much of her. Nevertheless, the horse needed her meds, so off I went.

I made my way around to most of the break-outs, greeting and welcoming people as I strolled. I love being the ambassador and Trinity's one-person cheerleading squad.

It was time for our first demonstration showcasing what we do here and how it helps veterans.

"Our horses aren't our tools — they're our partners. They're far more in tune with our intentions, emotions, and motivations than we give them credit for. A horse senses our struggles and encourages us to explore new perspectives and behaviors. They challenge us to trade our toxic mindsets for new beliefs and fresh paradigms," I explained.

My team and I were flooded with the number of ladies answering the invitation to join us in the arena and have an up-close and personal experience for themselves.

The questions were nonstop.

"Where should I stand?"

"Do they like it if you scratch their neck?"

"How can I tell if the horse likes me?"

"Can I ride this one?"

I stood back, lifting my voice only enough so all could hear.

"You all have really good questions. My team will answer them as you ask. But there's one most common question I'll answer upfront. You will not be riding today. The work we do with our horse partners is nearly all on the ground with them — shoulder-to-shoulder. That's where the connection starts and grows from. But you're welcome to keep filing in to brush and love on them," I finished.

I scanned the crowd looking for Sam. It took me a bit to subtly search the crowd of ladies clamoring to get their horse time.

But there she was, tucked in the corner by the tack locker, keeping company with the leftover cobwebs that got missed the day before. I signaled to one of our teammates to take my place as I left the arena and headed Sam's way.

"Are you finding things that interest you today?"

She replied, "My therapist suggested I try meditation or mindfulness, but it's impossible for me to turn off my thoughts. Doesn't do much good if you can't quiet your mind, does it?"

"I admit, that's a challenge." I nodded in agreement. "I started meditating years ago to get closer to God and hear Him better. Silencing my mind is a biggie," I confessed. "Where are you from? This event goes until 3 PM, but if you don't have to leave right away, I'd like to show you something that might help calm that mind of yours."

"I only live a few hours away. I'll see how I feel later and let you know."

"Fair enough."

It was heartwarming to see the ladies enjoying lunch together, sharing stories, and supporting each other with laughter and tearful hugs.

As the event was wrapping up, the female veterans made their final fly-byes to gather any remaining tips and materials from their favorite vendors.

For years, our tradition was to close this event by assembling next to the weathered shed with the American flag painted on it.

"Thank you all for being here. Thank you for your service and the sacrifices you made while supporting our country — state-side and abroad. We're proud of every single one of you. We hope you take what you've learned and enjoyed here today and put it into practice. Choose what moves the needle most for you. The ones that soothe your mind, body, and spirit. God bless you all."

I finished with a wave and sent them off.

They scattered like ants, hopping in their cars and leaving in parade fashion — except one. Samantha's car stood out like the Lone Ranger. But where was she?

While my team buttoned up the close-down details, I went on a hunt for Sam. I checked the typical places—the washroom, lounge, Grace Garden, the funnel, the round pen, and both the upper and lower barn. Nothing.

I decided to dash through the indoor arena to see if Sam snuck around the other way, and to my surprise, I saw her sitting on the therapeutic riding ramp.

"Hey, Sam. I'm so glad you stuck around."

"You said you'd show me something, so I was curious," she said nervously.

"Come on, let's go get the perfect horse for this."

"Do I have to do anything?"

"Not if you don't want to," I assured her.

I opened the gate, gave a quick whistle, and Bella lifted her head to begin her saunter towards us. Swaying from side to side, she met us at the water tank.

"Bella, meet Sam. Sam, meet Bella."

"She's ... she's beautiful," the veteran said in a soft, wispy voice.

As I opened the arena gate, the horse walked right in, turned around, and lowered her head. She knows the drill. We often remove the halter and begin with an activity, but not today. Not with this veteran.

I handed Bella's brush to Sam and said, "Start at her head and work your way to her tail. She likes the softness of the bristles."

"Am I pushing too hard? Am I hurting her?" she asked cautiously.

"Just watch her eyes. They'll tell you everything you need to know. How would you describe them?"

"Soft and calm looking. And when she looks at me, I can see the little folds on the edge that makes it look like she's smiling."

"That's because she is. She already knows you're a good person. She can tell by your gentle touch, your tone of voice, and your steady movements. All of those things make her feel safe and loved. You mentioned it was hard to quiet your head noise, to calm your mind. That's common with veterans like you who've seen combat," I explained.

I usually start with a breathing and grounding exercise, but not this time. I knew Sam had limited time, so I fast-forwarded to the *Hug* — The Rump Hug.

"I need you to trust me. I admit this is a bit unorthodox, but it's really helpful. You game?" I asked, trying to be reassuring at the same time.

Sam hesitantly agreed and followed my instructions to take the three steps up to the top of the mounting block. She swung her leg over the horse and squared herself on Bella's back.

"Now, this is the trust part. I'll hold your one leg while you swing the other one around, so you end up facing the horse's rear. It's okay. I've got you," I assured.

She obeyed.

"What emotions are bubbling up for you?" I asked.

"Uncomfortable, stressed, nervous, scared, kinda short of breath, and regretting I agreed to this," she said while shooting me a half-smile.

I remembered the comment about her asthma and assured her that all those feelings were normal and she was safe with me.

"Now, bend at the waist until your head and chest rest on the horse's back and rump."

"You're kidding, right? Put my head on the butt of a horse?"

"You said you trusted me. Don't give up on me now!" I challenged her. "Go ahead. Bella won't move a muscle. She knows what we're doing, and why."

The veteran slowly laid flat on Bella's rump. Her legs were tight and dog-leg shaped. Her hands were in a fist, and her eyes just stared at the ground.

"Take three really deep, big breaths. Inhale, hold it for a count of three, then exhale slow and long."

She did it but still looked stressed.

"Open your hands and let your arms relax, so they slide down on Bella's flanks. Relax your legs, so they just dangle. Soften every part of your body, then imagine you're a warm cozy blanket draped over Bella. Try to relive the feelings you had when you first saw this horse. I saw you. Your face was smooth, and your eyes were soft and dreamy."

About ten minutes passed before I noticed any change. But then I saw them. The tears rolled down Bella's rump. First, just a few, then a flood. Sam's body remained free and easy, so I considered the tears the good cleansing kind.

Thirty, forty, and even fifty minutes passed before I saw even a finger move.

"How are you doing, Sam?" I quietly whispered.

She slowly picked her head up and opened her eyes. Sam was wearing the most heavenly ear-to-ear smile.

"How was that for you?" I asked.

"That was magical. Simply magical," she said in a sing-song tone.

"What did you notice about your body, your breathing, your feelings?"

"I was calm, relaxed. My body felt limp, but in a good way. The only thing I heard was Bella's heart beating and her slow breaths in and out. Then I noticed the pace of our breathing matched. No sense of asthma for her or me and no shortness of breath. I felt content and confident — like my past was so far behind me that it had no control over me anymore. I was ME again. I *am* ME again — finally!"

"I'm so proud of you! You faced your fears and did it anyway. That's progress, my dear. That's how God works through us to help veterans find hope and healing. Amen, amen.

Father, the scripture Psalm 46:5 (NIV) comes to mind as we work with your female veterans. You say if You are within her, she will not fail. This is your promise to us all. You dwell within us, and we shall not fail. Thank You, Sweet Lord.

Author Note
Each state in the US has a separate Department of Veteran Affairs (DVA). The Wisconsin Department of Veteran Affairs, like all others, is a very good resource to educate resident veterans about their services, benefits, employment opportunities, and non-profit veteran-focused collaborators and affiliates they work with to provide the best possible support to its veterans.

And likewise, every county in every US state has its own County Veteran Service Officers (CVSOs). Their role is to be your advocate. To answer your questions, help you apply for and receive all the benefits you qualify for, and to put you in touch with the local or regional veteran-focused providers that will help support your individual needs. Most of the CVSOs are veterans themselves and have first-hand knowledge of how to navigate these processes successfully.

Take advantage of them. They really are waiting for you to stop in or call.

Chapter Eight
Crisis of Faith

We expect clergy to have all the answers. About life and death, salvation and damnation, good and evil—even heaven and hell. But what if it's the clergy who is asking the questions?

"Once we feel at ease enough to talk about the tough questions, we know we've wandered into a dangerous minefield. We call it a crisis of faith" (A.A.W. US Army Chaplain).

The job of a combat chaplain is to bring God to men, and men to God.

"A war zone is a complex place, filled with ambiguities, conflicting interpretations, and unanswerable questions. It's a continuous balancing act for a chaplain. My faith is constantly under fire" (A.R.H. – US Army Chaplain).

"The stress of a combat zone becomes unbearable. It changes you. Like when someone takes 20-grit sandpaper to a beautiful table. At first, you hardly notice the marks it leaves. But with more pressure, the groves dig deeper, wearing through its protective layers, and exposing the raw, unprotected insides. It will never be the same. Neither will I. It can send you into a tailspin, like an F-16 plunging towards a crash" (B.F.S. USAF Chaplain).

Frank discovered his divine DNA at six-years-old, while holding church services for his young neighborhood congregants. Now in his seventies, this career military Chaplain held countless worship services for his fellow unit members.

"Soldiers and airmen expected me to comfort and guide them. But instead, I pacified them with platitudes, cleverly disguising my own questions and doubts," Frank said.

Doubt is dangerous. It can deteriorate our devotion to the truth and alter our perception of right and wrong. But questions, especially those that measure your morals and ethics, can haunt you for a lifetime.

"What if it was *you* who was faced with an unconscionable choice? What if you were the combat veteran who did and saw things never to be undone? What if you had to choose between survival or humanity, knowing no matter your choice, you're destined to live tormented by the other."

He continued, "It's what happens when the mighty promises of our faith have a head-on collision with the cruel, unjust, and inhumane happenings of our life."

Tayna, the chaplain's wife of over fifty years, looked utterly bored as Frank began recalling their many adventures crisscrossing the globe. Her attitude grew to disdain as he described how God used him in mighty ways.

She eventually erupted. "See, this is what drives me crazy. I was as involved as he was, only in a different way. But nobody appreciated that. Nobody even heard about that."

Normally God makes it crystal clear to us who He wants helped, and why. Not this time. Was it Frank with his years of behind-the-lines exposure to death and destruction? Or Tayna, who lived a lifetime in the enormous shadow of a beloved military chaplain, with no voice to speak of?

We began our first equestrian session with Jazzy waiting in the arena. The mare was a working girl. An old, retired Reiner who appreciated a savvy rider and steady handler. The chaplain was neither.

"Frank, let's have you greet the horse, and use the lead rope to bring her to us."

"Oh, no ma'am, I couldn't do that," the veteran replied. "I don't want to seem uncooperative, but I've hurt enough people and creatures by not doing my job well, and I vowed never to hurt another living thing."

It took the team numerous attempts to convince him a soft rope around the horse's neck wouldn't cause pain. He finally agreed to try. Sort of.

Jazzy stood perfectly still while Frank finally followed our instructions. Jazzy didn't change her demeanor. Chappy insisted, "See, she doesn't like it. Jazzy won't come with me."

I calmly instructed, "Just pick up the rope, give it a little tug, and she'll know you want her to follow."

Frank teared up, maintaining I was wrong, and it was inhumane.

Tayna charged in from the sidelines, as if we had called for a relief pitcher. "For heaven sakes man, just grab the darn rope, give it a tug, and she'll follow you. You're in charge, so do your job. If you were a leader, you'd have told those young boys what they were walking into. Not you. You thought your prayers were enough."

Horses have "tells," just like poker players. Only the equine versions aren't nearly as subtle. Horses tell us they're angry or offended by narrowing their eyes, pinning their ears, whipping their tails, and pounding the ground. Jazzy told us, in no uncertain terms, the session was over.

As Tayna stormed out, Frank spoke up. "She's right, you know. It was my fault they died. Seven of them." He plopped down on the mounting block and kept talking. "We received intel of ambushes reported in our region. Credible intel. My job was to emotionally and spiritually prepare the troops. It wasn't to read them in on details, expectations, or projections. I knew my unit might take fire. If true, I knew some probably wouldn't survive. But I didn't say anything. I didn't prepare them for that."

While my partner consoled Frank, I concentrated on Jazzy. Sometimes she seems more human than horse. She slowly walked up behind the chaplain and stood unnoticed for moments while Frank pulled himself together. Then the horse softly rested her nose on the vet's shoulder. Frank was startled at first, but then without warning, threw his arms around the horse's neck, buried his face in her mane, and sobbed.

Most horses are naturally affectionate, but not Jazzy. She's known to be unapproachable, aloof, and even unfriendly. Jazzy would rather walk away from sentiment than stand for it. Ironically, that's what makes this horse the perfect therapy partner. We trusted that when she did something, it was because she wanted to, not because she was trying to please us.

We watched as Jazzy stood statue still, absorbing the chaplain's tears, grief, and regrets. The connection between the two was authentic. *Eureka, here we go!*

The following week Frank bounced in, smiling from ear to ear. Tayna was MIA. We asked, "Is your wife joining us today?"

"Nope. She said I could come by myself."

We needed to test the resilience of Frank's recent eureka moment. To see if the connection was durable.

"Let's have you untie Jazzy and lead her around the arena."

Old habits die hard. The veteran started his excuses and refusals, so it was time for a push.

I untied the horse's rope and gave it to the chaplain, leaving him no other choice but to take it. "Now, off you go. Your horse is waiting for you to become the leader God created you to be."

Jazzy abruptly pulled Frank from his standstill and started the lesson on her own. The chaplain looked frightened, lagging behind her, and finally stopped altogether.

"Nope, I won't do this. Jazzy doesn't like it, and I won't force her."

Before we had time to answer his refusals, the horse pulled hard, jerking the rope from Frank's hand, and moving ahead without him. She stopped, took a half-turn towards him, clearly waiting for him to catch up. When he did, the horse walked off again. This cat and mouse game continued for nearly twenty minutes.

Finally, Frank understood. The horse wasn't going to take NO for an answer. This chaplain was going to become a leader, period. Frank walked a step ahead of her, staying in pace, but a leader all the same.

Now it was test time. "Unclip the rope and see if she'll follow you." It was a gamble, but if I read the horse right, it would catapult Frank's healing into orbit.

Sure enough, Jazzy followed Frank's lead. Every turn, every speed change, every stop, start, and pause. They were in perfect tandem. The veteran was in heaven.

Finishing up, we saw Tayna peeking through the arena blinds. We motioned for her to join us, but she answered by mouthing an over exaggerated *NO!*

As we entered the lounge and greeted her, Frank chattered non-stop about the success of his session. His wife was less than impressed.

"I'm only here to pick him up, not to hear how good he is. I'm full up on that."

As the hostility continued, we were convinced it was God's plan to help them both. A holy "twofer," we concluded. But private sessions. Fewer wounds that way.

Tayna arrived ten minutes early for her appointment. She sat frozen, arms crossed and head down, as if she was waiting to see the principal.

Gate five was home to Ronnie, a recent rag-tag little rescued mare who spent the last several years isolated before she came to us, with only a twice-a-week delivery of two flakes of hay and a splash of water. It was enough to keep her physically alive, but she was emotionally dying. The horse was miles out of her element, with no way for us to prepare her for Trinity's sixty-seven acres of horses, staff, visitors, and action. She was terrified.

As we entered the pasture, we saw a smile crease Tayna's face for the first time. She pointed to Ronnie saying, "What's her story? She looks like I feel—beaten, bruised, and broken."

I explained, "She's new to Trinity, trying to find her place and identity."

Tayna was noticeably excited, asking, "Can I work with her?"

"Of course, but don't be surprised if you can't get near her. She's never learned to trust horses or humans," I warned.

Then Tayna did something totally unexpected, yet brilliant. Instead of walking directly towards the horse, she spotted a stump near the horse, sat down, propped her head in her hands, and patiently waited.

We stood back, marveling at the wife's success as we watched the horse zig-zag her way to check out the stranger on the stump. Tayna slowly stretched her hand out, reaching for the horse, while Ronnie leaned to her limit, trying to touch the woman's hand with her nose. It reminded me of Michelangelo's famous painting, "The Creation of Adam." With one single touch, a consecrated connection was created between God and Man, and between Tayna and Ronnie.

For the next several months, we continued separate sessions for Frank and Tayna. Their independent work with Jazzy and Ronnie was invaluable in their independent healing journeys, but it was time for a meeting of the minds and hearts.

The horses reacted first. Their rearing, snorting, and bucking told us they were wildly unhappy with the meeting plans. The couple stood separated by the training pedestal in the center of the arena.

We were thinking it, but Frank said it. "Looks like us, doesn't it, Tayna? Arguing and getting angry with each other." She didn't react. Frank poked more. "Really, this is how our marriage has felt for years."

His wife exploded. "I love God too, you know. I had a calling on my life that was just as important as yours. But you never wanted to hear about that, did you? You thought everything was about you. The great and glorious Frank. All you wanted from me was a hot supper, and a clean uniform."

The horses stopped bickering, and trotted to stand quietly next to their human partners. Tayna continued her rant, while Ronnie worked her muzzle under the woman's elbow, sharply nudging her. The horse continued, even though Tayna was trying her hardest to ignore it. After the third or fourth strong jab, Tayna realized her partner was trying to tell her something— remind her of something.

Frank's wife stopped her attack, took a deep breath, and remembered the many hours she spent with Ronnie building their relationship. Tayna vividly related the session when she chose to stop being defensive and angry, and start being honest, open, and willing to own her part in the unraveling of their marriage.

The wife softened her voice and confessed, "I only said that about the boys in your unit and your prayers to hurt you. Like I felt you'd hurt me." She went on, "After a while, I just stopped caring. About you, our work, and our marriage. You just kept going, like nothing was wrong. You never saw what I was experiencing. You never heard me crying at night. Or maybe you did and didn't care."

Frank softly replied, "I heard you crying. I knew you were hurting, but I just didn't know what to say or do. I'm so sorry, Tayna. You are and have always been my rock. My partner."

It took months, but Frank finally became comfortable leading Jazzy to all corners of the ranch. He still insisted on consoling and apologizing to Jazzy as they went on their walks. Only now, it was with a smile and a chuckle knowing he was needling us.

On the other hand, to watch Tayna work with Ronnie was like witnessing Mother Teresa tend to the ill and broken. Her compassion and patience were tireless. The bond created between the two ladies stirred Tayna deeply, while transforming Ronnie.

"Ronnie makes me wonder if my calling all along was to help the other wives," Tayna sweetly said.

"What other wives?" I inquired.

"The droves I've met over the years, and across the globe. The ones just like me who believed they didn't matter and had nothing to contribute. That everything was about their husband's calling. *Those* wives."

"What would you tell them if you could?"

"I'd tell them they're valuable, anointed, and equal partners to their husbands, not just their shadows. I'd tell them God never intended for them to live as a silhouette, but instead to step into their own glory, and shine. To be who He called them to be—right alongside their husbands. I'd tell them that's how they'll live out their calling."

By the end of our time together, Jazzy and Ronnie grew to be close allies, and were instrumental in helping heal the couple's wounds.

"The horses taught us how to be fearless. That changed everything," Frank proudly shared. "They taught us to be fearlessly honest, fearlessly vulnerable, and fearlessly forgiving."

Ultimately, the retired chaplain went on to write his memoir, chronicling the many lessons he treasured from his military service, his service to God, and his service to Tayna, his ministry partner.

And as it turned out, Tayna was a bit of a writer herself. She launched a very successful blog that encouraged and mentored hundreds of "those wives" from around the world. She helped them find their voice, their passion, and their light, so they could shine for Jesus.

Lord, thank You for forgiving our doubts and fears. We will not allow the evil one to shake the foundation of our beliefs, values, or commitment to You.

In the name of Jesus Christ, we declare – we are fearless, unapologetically devoted to You. Thank You for proclaiming; WE ARE YOURS.

Author Note

I'm a book nut. I love reading them, studying them, highlighting any key thoughts and ideas, dog-earring the pages that I don't want to lose sight of, writing in the margins, and of course, dating the comments. So it only makes sense that when times get tough, and the wheels on my life's wagon wobble, I go to my bookshelf to lean on my favorite authors who have compassionately propped me up over the years, and through the tears.

My eyes shop my shelf for just the right title that speaks truth into my trials, puts out my raging fire of uncertainty, and tames the giants that threaten to eat me alive. Or at least it feels like it.

My Top 10 favorite truth-tellers, fire extinguishers, and sword-carrying heroes are; Max Lucado, Dr. Brene' Brown, Joyce Meyers, Tim Storey, Phillip Yancey, Mark Batterson, John Eldridge, Richard Rohr, and John Ortberg.

Chapter Nine
Obstacles That Free You

"When man plans, God laughs." I've thought of this old Yiddish proverb many times as we plan our veteran sessions. We try to think two steps ahead of the client and the horse. To anticipate the probable obstacles and outcomes.

Over the years, and after enduring many stutter-starts and unexpected endings, we gladly admit we are not in control of our sessions. You may think that sounds unprofessional, even unsafe.

But what if I told you that instead of planning our steps, insisting the session go in a specific direction, we step back, stand down, and leave the plan, the pace, and the particulars to God?

We don't presume an outcome or follow patterns of past sessions. It's actually so relieving to let "Jesus take the wheel" or the reins. It's how the Divine directs the directable. That's the secret – being directable, teachable, guidable. That came in real handy when we took on Harold and Nan.

We greeted them as they stepped out of their worn and rusted 4-door Buick. Neither said much, but Nan threw us a glimpse of a smile. Harold's head was down as he asked, "So where do we go to get this stuff rolling?"

Our standard rule is for our therapy team to sit closest to the door for safety reasons. A quick escape if need be. Normally this is the same place our veterans prefer to sit, for the same reason. Not this time.

Harold rattled off, "I'll only stay in here if I can sit where I can see the door. I startle easily and need to see what's coming."

Great. But what did he mean about startling "easily"?

We should have repaired it years ago. The door between the indoor arena and the hallway had an auto-close feature, but didn't have the brakes that cushioned the slam.

BAM! Harold jumped out of his chair, pointed an invisible rifle at the conference room door, and began making very loud shooting sounds. It took him several minutes to regain his composure and emotionally return to the room. To this moment in time, and to this meeting.

Harold's startle response was off the Richter scale. My heart went out to him. You could see how he was terrified and embarrassed. I profusely apologized to him and jotted a note to have our maintenance man fix the door immediately.

We tried to gather his attention by asking what branch of service he was in, his role, how long, anything that might help ground him.

"I was a grunt, but did the work of my CO. He was a fool, and couldn't make a decision to save his life, or ours. Repeatedly, I bailed our unit out by taking control, and becoming the leader."

I was sitting there wondering if that was even possible with the rigidity of the roles and structure of military missions. But if so, what an incredible conflict that likely caused between Harold and his higher-ups.

"Even though I saved our guys more than once, there was that one time..." He trailed off.

"That one time?" I asked.

Harold sat back in his chair, tightly folded his arms, and began to mumble to himself.

A direct question was not going to give us what we needed. "Thanks for that information, Harold. Let's head out to the pasture and see the horses. Nan, will you be joining us?"

"Oh no, this is Harold's time. I've heard his stories. Now it's your turn. I told him, but I'll tell you ladies too, if this doesn't work, I'm done."

Nan continued, "I'm done making excuses for him. Done living like a hermit, and done being afraid of his PTSD. It's been over half his life since this all happened, but he lives it every day. I've decided I don't have to anymore. I won't." She left the room to wait in the car.

We entered gate five, the home to many of our therapy horses. As I latched the gate behind us and began walking down the center of the pasture, we turned to engage Harold, but he wasn't there. He was still next to the closed gate, watching. I quickly rejoined him, thinking he might have a fear of horses that hadn't been expressed.

He said, "I prefer to just watch them before I join in."

Hmmm, that's insightful.

It surprised us when he stated, "I don't want to know their names, or their stories—yet. They don't know mine, so I shouldn't know theirs. Not until one chooses me."

We let Harold lead by a few steps. Behind him, my therapy partner and I exchanged puzzled glances and raised eyebrows. I pointed to the sky, with a slight head tilt, as if to say, *We plan, God laughs—again.*

It figured. Harold pointed to the most withdrawn, fear-filled mare on the entire ranch. The veteran walked slower than slow, as if he was operating under the radar. The other horses approached him, but he politely dismissed them as he continued his path to her.

For a man who struggles with "a scrambled brain," he seemed remarkably in the moment. In tune to his body and pace, the sounds his clothing was making, and the horse's reaction to it all.

Star was a tall, lankly, jet-black mare with a crispy white star on her forehead that was so perfect, people assumed it was hand-painted. We don't know her entire story, but it was obvious she preferred to be alone, not needing friendships, support, or mending. Or so she thought.

No wonder Harold chose this horse. As so often happens, without knowing it, veterans choose the horse with a similar story to theirs.

He got within ten feet of the horse, and she bolted off. Star stopped, turned, and glared at him. Harold didn't move. Not out of fear, but insistence and defiance, it appeared. Harold demanded this encounter go his way. He didn't care if Star felt the same or not. His way or no way.

Harold turned and headed for the gate.

"Do you want to meet a different horse?" I asked.

"Nope. She's the one. She just doesn't know it yet."

The following week, he arrived alone. We met him outside and asked, "No Nan today?"

"I don't need her to do what I have to do today," he growled.

What he needed to do today? That sounded ominous, and even a little scary.

Harold blew into the lounge, down the hallway to the barn, out the back door, and into gate five. As usual, Star was alone, with her back to the fence line, facing what would be coming at her. Sound familiar?

Harold's pace wasn't nearly as smooth as the previous week. He hustled towards the horse, pushing into an engagement, only to have her and her 1100 pounds push back.

Star charged off, turned, and began the stare-down of all stare-downs. The horse added a few foot stomps, tail swishes, and shrill snorts to shout her point.

Harold recited, "I would rather have her respect than her compliance. Her trust in me, rather than her intimidation by me. I would rather have her friendship than her contempt. Therefore, I will bend, I will change, and I will be what she needs me to be."

WOW! Where did that come from?

It was like some kind of horsey hocus pocus spell he cast over Star. I handed him the halter and lead, and he quietly draped it over her face as she lowered her head to accept it. What?

We headed to the obstacle arena. Tall stumps, water elements, teetering wooden bridges, huge boulders, felled trees, all arranged in a strategic, and challenging course to maneuver. This horse had never encountered the course. Actually, she had never even seen this side of the ranch.

The vet tightened his grip on the lead, as the horse began to side-step and resist. Wondering if Harold was feeling out of his comfort zone, I asked if he'd rather I took her.

He confidently replied, "No, she needs to know I'm not afraid, so she won't be afraid."

Amen, brother! That's exactly how horses learn who's the leader, and who can or cannot be trusted. Harold was spot on.

Star trotted into the arena with Harold matching her pace. He gently but firmly pulled back on her lead rope until she stopped, talking to her as if she understood every word.

"Hey girl, I've never been in here before either. But no matter what, I'll protect you." He had me hold the horse's lead rope while walking the course by himself. He wanted to prove to Star, and himself, that everything was okay.

He was clearly nervous and seemed to be triggered by the bridge and tall stumps he couldn't see around. He listened to our instructions and how the course was to be maneuvered, but emphatically refused to follow them.

From his spot on the course, Harold shouted, "This is how people get killed! Following a known route is what the enemy expects you to do. I will not take my horse through a hot zone and invite an ambush."

He came back in a huff, grabbed Star's lead, and they began. Harold talked to the horse the entire way, explaining his new route and the reason for it. He stopped at the bridge and tried to hide his tears, but gave up as he began sobbing.

Harold took Star's head in his hands and finally spoke about the horrific things that haunted him. The veteran told in detail his attempts to save his unit when the CO ran in fear. He described how the sounds, explosions, and bombs going off were deafening. Everything shook until it crumbled.

Both the veteran and horse chose to stop the journey for the day. It was a meeting of the minds, with a pledge to pick it up another day.

We spent the next hour helping Harold settle his nerves, but still within sight of the obstacle arena. My partner, the therapist of our team, whispered that staying within view of the bridge was a method of desensitizing the veteran to its presence, and diminishing its power. It would help calm his emotions and put the past back where it belonged — in the past.

It was weeks before Harold believed either he or Star was ready for another try at the course. We still don't know what changed, but trusted God's timing.

We talked as we walked out to Star's pasture. We asked what he thought would be different this time. How could we support him in the process? Support Star? Why did he feel today was the day?

He didn't have answers for most, but he said, "I just know today was OUR day." Harold didn't share why, but he exuded absolute confidence.

We reached the end of the barn, swung the door open, and there she was, standing at the gate. Star was waiting for Harold, giving him a soft nicker, pawing the ground to show her enthusiasm.

We wondered if somehow the veteran saw the horse waiting at the gate, and that's where he got the idea that today would be successful. But we quickly agreed there's no way Harold could have seen Star before we reached the back door. It was impossible for him to know she was waiting.

The vet broke into a belly laugh saying, "Ha, even *she* knows today's our day! She knows it!"

He haltered Star and they walked to the same arena. The veteran insisted on creating a new route. "It's a different day, so there has to be a different route. It's safer that way."

They were making great progress until reaching the bridge. Star stopped first, then Harold. Both stood motionless, neither making any effort to move forward.

The vet let the lead rope slip through his fingers and fall to the ground. He climbed the three steps it took to reach the top of the bridge platform and planted himself. He stood as if he'd just reached the summit of Mount Kilimanjaro. Proud, confident, and beaming with satisfaction. Not a danger in sight.

Star was at the base of the steps. She was clearly unsure about Harold's request for her to join him on the platform. The vet reached down to grab her lead, then stepped back, giving her ample space on the bridge, and kissed to her.

"Come on girl, you can do this. I wouldn't ask you if I wasn't sure it was safe. You can trust me. Remember this is our day. Today is it!"

He took a step towards the edge of the wooden platform and asked her again.

To our surprise, the horse skipped the process of walking up the stairs, and leaped onto the floor space, planting all fours right next to Harold. Both horse and human soaked up the moment, reveling in the horse's Olympic-like, four-point, gold medal landing, as we recognized the monumental progress that happened right before our eyes.

Harnessing adrenaline and confidence, they continued meeting each obstacle with ease and in any order they wanted. Walking towards them, coming up from behind, side-stepping the ground poles, and backing up the entire length of the course.

It was proof that our barriers aren't always things that block our way or prevent our progress. Instead, if we allow them, they can be the God-led inspiration for life-changing progress. They can be the obstacles that free you and me. Freeing us by allowing for an equine assisted recovery, and divinely planned redemption.

What an amazing God you are. What an amazing Father, friend, guide, and driver of our lives You are. Thank You for living life right next to us, hand-in-hand, step-by-step. Thank You for taking the plans we make and transforming them into what You need them to be, for us and all those we serve, to live the life you created us for.

Author Note

One of my favorite songs is by a country singer made famous as a winner of likely the largest talent contest program in the world.

The singer shares how she and her baby daughter were traveling back home on a cold wintery Christmas Eve. There was only an hour or so to go, but she was tired and the roads were slippery. Instead of focusing to stay safe, she was toiling over her past, was going too fast, hit a patch of black ice and went into a horrifying spin, landing in the ditch.

Their life flashed before them, and in desperation she cried out, asking Jesus to take the wheel. Not just of her car, but of her life. She confessed she's made bad choices and can't do this life on her own. She needs His help. She prays for forgiveness and promises from that moment on she gives Him control.

The song ends there, but as we know, that's just the beginning. When we ask—God answers. He steps in, but only after we ask. He doesn't wait because He enjoys seeing us struggle, but because He refuses to push Himself on us.

In Revelation 3:20, it tells us that Jesus stands at the door of *our heart* and knocks. He tells us if we can hear His voice and if we're willing to open the door, He'll come in and share a meal together as friends.

In our equine therapy work, we use metaphors as a tool to help better understand the revelations that take place. Clearly that thread leads all the way back to biblical times. Meal is His metaphor for life.

Jesus stands at the door of our hearts, softly calling our name, and waiting—waiting for us to accept His invitation do life together with Him. He celebrates and never, ever refuses when we ask Him to *take the wheel.*

There is no safer driver.

Chapter Ten
Lie Detector

The truth is—we can't help every veteran. Sometimes our method isn't a good fit for the client, and sometimes the client isn't a good fit for our method. However, nine chances out of ten, it's the fit that changes, and sometimes saves their life.

"A good fit" for the veteran before us was yet to be determined.

This multi-decorated, four-time deployed Army veteran had worn bare any friendship he'd ever valued, burned every bridge he'd ever crossed, and was working at setting a blaze to the one he was currently standing on with us.

Whether it was drugs, alcohol, adrenaline, poisonous relationships, chronic lying, or manipulation—he used it, wanted it, needed it, and would trade, or steal anything for it.

Even his mother wasn't immune to this veteran's in-home robberies. It infuriated her when he stole money from her purse, looted her medicine cabinet, and *used* her car after it had been forbidden.

But what stung the most was his lying to her face.

Being an arms specialist demanded an intensity of focus and level of courage few are required to have, and even fewer have to prove it daily.

Jamie considered his military world of high-performance and high-stakes life as living *the life*. Without it, he'd search out any edgy activity that would give him even a momentary thrill.

Hunter was a mild-mannered, middle-aged gelding that "hunted" for the discrepancies in an encounter. His superpower was unearthing lies, half-truths, and the occasional camouflaged bait and switch.

This horse rightfully earned the nickname LD—Lie Detector.

When a client tried to rewrite their rap sheet or lead us down a bunny trail, Hunter would sniff it out, and spill the beans.

If our client is honest, it shortcuts the therapeutic process and instantly gives us something to work with. If not, we waste time sorting and sifting.

Knowing truthfulness is not guaranteed, rules are necessary.

Drugs and weapons top Trinity's prohibition list. Handguns, knives, street drugs, overuse of prescribed drugs, or a belly full of alcohol are all banned and earn you an escort to the door.

Jamie came for a *visit* to see if "we were the kind of help he was looking for."

He stretched back in the chair, crossed his arms, and said, "So tell me what you do here."

Matching his tone, I replied, "Just curious, have you looked at our website? Have you read anything about us?"

Every new veteran teaches us something—even after the three hundredth one.

They help us grow our *street smarts* and learn more and more about the head and heart of a veteran.

Those *smarts* tell us that no veteran would step into an unfamiliar environment without first doing some recon. They'd never set themselves up for an ambush like that.

We proceeded, believing Jamie had looked us up, knew who we were, what we did, and how we did it.

Let the games begin.

"How about we reschedule this appointment and give you time to look into the work we do here. To see if it's a good fit," I said, calling his bluff.

"Nah, that won't be necessary. I already looked you over," he confessed, with an air of superiority. "You think I'd come here without checking you out?"

Normally, we'd finish our paperwork and take the new client on a facility tour. Not this time. Within moments of the assessment starting, my therapy partner gave me the "caution" signal, so I knew to wrap it up.

"It was good to meet you, Jamie. Is there a day next week where you could come back for a tour and meet some horses?" I asked.

"No," he said dismissively. "I'm good with it. Let's just start."

"We do have to follow our protocols. What day next week works for you?" I repeated.

The reason for postponing the tour was to slow down this runaway train. We needed time to decide if we felt comfortable moving forward or not.

"And when you come back, would you please lock your handgun in the trunk of your car?" I said, pointing to the handle poking out of his pocket.

"You must have missed the sign on the door stating no weapons allowed," my therapy partner said.

The veteran left with next week's appointment in the books, along with instructions to wear closed-toed shoes. We like everyone to go home with their toes intact. An accidental side-step from a 1500 pound horse can change that in a hurry.

Normally, we don't review the new client's file. While sometimes helpful, the therapist I work with prefers to see how the client presents. She doesn't want to see the diagnosis, the behavioral labels, or the conjectures and summaries.

But this time felt different. This veteran felt different. Our need to know what we were getting into trumped our long-held use of therapeutic blinders.

"His file mentioned *possible* borderline personality disorder that could *possibly* be exacerbated by his PTSD. It also noted a pathology of lying and *possible* narcissism," she said, with a hard exhale. "That's a whole lot of *possibles* for one person."

I agreed with her.

"By the look of his eyes, he was definitely on something," the therapist added. "Not sure it was only the alcohol we could smell, or if there was something else adding to his attitude."

"It could all be a clever smoke screen," I said.

The therapist paused, resting her hand on her chin. "Could be he's none of these things. Just using them as a shield. A shield to keep people second guessing so they won't dive into the real issues."

"Or…it could be self-sabotage," I added. "He's a smart guy. Maybe he thinks being uncooperative would disqualify him from our program, making us the bad guys for not helping him."

The therapist closed the file. "Either way, let's be ready to move forward."

When we wonder if a client is suitable for our program, we enlist our horses to help tip the scale.

Back in the day, when horses ran wild, their life depended on their ability to accurately assess their environment, and those in it. Then, as now, a horse's skill remains remarkably reliable in this area.

Within an arm's length, a horse can feel how fast a human heart is beating. A fast beat can mean anxious, untrusting, and even untruthful. Slow—grounded, calm, and open.

That information creates a baseline. From there, the horse scrutinizes the most minute shifts in the veteran's body language.

The horse's findings are disclosed by how he interacts with the client. This process gives us an enormous advantage by knowing if the veteran is likely trustworthy or not.

The week blew by, and it was only moments before Jamie would arrive. Or so we thought.

Twenty-five minutes later, the veteran sauntered in wearing jet black sunglasses and his hood pulled so low it nearly touched his nose.

Eyes tell us so much. We couldn't help but wonder what he was hiding.

I greeted him as I would with any of our vets. "Good morning, Jamie. It's good to see you again."

"Will you please remove your sunglasses?" my therapy partner requested. "I'd like us all to feel comfortable."

"Looks like you missed our reminder to be safe and wear closed-toed shoes," I said.

"No, I heard you. But…I guess I forgot." Jamie shrugged his shoulders.

"Now you get to make a choice. We have extra boots for you to use today, or you can go home and get your shoes."

"Or we'll postpone this session, and you can come back next week with closed-toes shoes," I said, without a hint of negotiation.

"What'll it be, Jamie?"

"They're in my car," he said while getting up.

Could he have forgotten his shoes were in his car? Sure. But did he? Or was this another play for control?

Hunter was waiting for us at the gate when we entered the indoor arena.

We handed Jamie a curry brush, asked him to introduce himself to the horse, and to give him a friendly brushing.

My eyes were glued to the two.

Jamie started by telling the gelding about the missions he led—debugging this, and defusing that. It was impossible to tell if the yarn he was spinning was true, or just being spun.

But Hunter told us.

The horse put his forehead on the vet's shoulder and gave it a shove.

That's his *tell*. That's how Hunter tells us the client's lying.

Jamie kept talking without realizing the horse's actions. The vet just moved further from Hunter's range, and kept on.

The horse walked back up to the veteran and gave him another shove, only stronger this time.

Finally, Jamie noticed the horse's action, raised his voice, and said, "Hey bud, knock it off, or I'll give it right back to you."

Hunter stepped back, turned, and squared off. The horse knew what was next.

We handed Jamie a lead rope, and instructed him to take the horse on a walk around the arena.

Horses can be persnickety. They won't follow just anyone.

If they do, it's because they think you're trustworthy—a leader.

Jamie started off assuming the horse would automatically be in tow, and was miffed when he noticed Hunter refused.

The vet turned toward the horse and spewed a litany of choice words in frustration. Hunter clearly didn't approve. He came up to Jamie and gave him a hard shove, nearly upending him.

"Why does he keep doing that?" Jamie shouted. "I've had enough of it!"

I spoke up, "It's been our experience that when this horse does that thing, he's telling us there's a discrepancy between your insides and outsides. In simpler terms, Jamie, the horse is telling us you're being untruthful—you're lying."

"That's BS," he said. "No horse can tell if someone's lying."

"Oh, quite the contrary," my therapy partner chimed in. This horse can detect a lie just by being close to the one who's lying. Then he uses his shoulder shove to tell us."

"He's a lie detector. No straps or gauges needed for him," I said.

"He's never failed us yet." The therapist pivoted so she was face-to-face with the veteran, and sincerely asked, "Jamie, do you want to be here? Do you want to work with horses to help manage your PTSD? Or, is showing up late, *forgetting* your shoes, disregarding our rules, and your lies a way to get expelled from our program?"

Jamie was noticeably surprised by the frankness of the question.

His tough-guy exterior softened as he stared at the ground and confessed, "I don't know. I got problems, that's for sure. But I'm not sure you could help me, even if I wanted you to."

"That's where you need to start. You first need to decide if you want to get better," the therapist said. "Then you decide who or what method you think would be your best fit."

"But if I talk about everything I saw, I'm afraid the nightmares will get even worse."

"Being afraid is normal," my partner empathized. "Sometimes it does get worse before it gets better."

"But Jamie, it does get better—if you're honest," I said.

"So...if I tell you everything, do you think you can help me?"

I knew I spoke for both my therapy partner and myself when I said, "We'll do our best."

"Okay, let's start over," Jamie said as he straightened.

The moment the vet came clean, the horse walked over and quietly stood by his side.

Jamie smiled, cocked his head, and pointed to Hunter. "Looks like he knows I'm gonna be honest."

We all stood in the middle of the arena while Jamie shared his military experience. He told us the reason he uses drugs and "bathes in alcohol."

"I can't shake the memory of what we found when we were clearing enemy bunkers," he said with a shaky voice. "At first we couldn't see anything. It was so dark inside. But then I panned from wall to wall with my flashlight—and we saw it."

Shaking as he continued, Jamie said, "There were chains and hooks hanging from the walls. It took us a minute, but then we realized this enemy bunker was used to torture our troops." His voice caught in his throat. "Some of the hooks still had... *proof* hanging from them."

Our throats tightened too.

"The smell, what we saw—and what we didn't see but could imagine—was sickening. I just can't shake that vision," Jamie said, his voice trailing off.

The veteran went on to describe, in even more detail, two other bunkers they found with similar evidence.

No wonder he couldn't forget.

From that day on, the veteran showed up on time, was respectful and cooperative, and never suffered another shoulder shove.

We worked with Jamie for the better part of a year, meeting nearly every week. We grew to look forward to our sessions with him and enjoyed watching the vet and the horse become close allies.

When our time together came to a close, Jamie shared the many things Hunter taught him about himself.

"That horse helped me sort through *why I did what I did*. And the activities helped me understand how important *the pause* is, and why I need to use it to think before I do."

Gratitude consumed me over the progress he'd made.

"Hunter taught me what trust looks like—and feels like. He taught me that my past doesn't need to control my present, or future. That facing my past is part of the process, and it helps create my progress."

"That's it, Jamie."

"I now know it's *me* who has the power to defuse it—just like I did with the bombs. I believe I'm on my way to being a good person. A person who can be trusted. A person my mom would be proud to call her son."

What more could we have hoped for with this once habitual liar?

"And I'm so thankful you taught me how God sees me. Not like a failure or a bad person — but someone He lovingly calls son. What I've learned from this horse and this place is priceless," Jamie said.

Father, You are so patient with us. Even when we're defiant, deceitful, and disrespectful, You still love us and still forgive us. Thank You for rebuilding our character from the inside out. In Jesus' name we pray. Amen.

Author Note

The way we often see ourselves isn't remotely close to how God sees us or thinks of us.

Take a look at how Scripture shapes it:
- ❖ You were wonderfully made (Psalms 139:14, Ephesians 2:10, Genesis 1:27)
- ❖ You are extremely valuable (Matthew 6:26, Luke 12:7, Psalms 139:1-4)
- ❖ You are continually on His mind (Jeremiah 29:11, Psalms 139:17-18)
- ❖ He never leaves your side (Joshua 1:9, Matthew 28:20)
- ❖ You were created for a purpose (Jeremiah 1:5, Ephesians 1:11)
- ❖ You are royalty and heirs (1 Peter 2:9, Galatians 3:26, Galatians 4:7)
- ❖ He deeply cares about your wellbeing (1 Peter 5:6-7, Matthew 6:25-26)
- ❖ God loves you very much (John 3:16, Isaiah 43:4, Romans 5:8, John 15:13)
- ❖ He has a precious gift for you (Acts 2:38, Ephesians 1:7)

Chapter Eleven
God's Amazing Grace

"St. Michael, the Archangel, defend us in battle. Be our defense against the wickedness and snares of the devil."

When Claudia enlisted and was nominated to attend the famed United States Military Academy—West Point—she thought her path was securely set. But this veteran's nightly prayers ended with her petition to St. Michael seeking protection not over foreign enemies, but over the enemies within her own unit.

Claudia was tougher and stronger than most cadets—even the male cadets. She was a female on a mission to excel, to break records, and to change the perception of women in high-ranking positions in the US Army.

Her acumen was generally seen as admirable and valorous.

But not by all. A small group of male cadets saw Claudia as a threat. A threat she may surpass them in rank, eclipse their achievements, mock their manhood, and degrade their domination.

As she left her final appointment of the evening and crossed campus to return to her barracks, she was approached by two unfamiliar male cadets.

She put her head down and tried to plow her way around them, but they created a road-block, forcing her to stop. The men physically restrained her, pushing her back and forth between them, calling her vulgar names and taunting her to fight back.

"You think you're special, don't you? That you won't get our best just because you're so smart and strong?"

The men became more aggressive as they ripped her uniform.

They took turns assaulting her.

⚜ ⚜ ⚜

When it was over, the male cadets scattered while Claudia tried to collect herself. She staggered back to the barracks.

This female cadet told no one.

Not fighting back seemed cowardice to her. She was probably stronger than they were. But her training in deescalating and assessing threats told her there was nothing she could've said or done that would have spared her from what happened.

Graduation came and went. Active Duty Deployment Cycles ramped up and closed—but not without incident.

Lt. Col. Claudia Warninger held her head high as she received a commendation for being an outstanding leader, trainer, and motivator.

As proud as she was, she still felt the sting of the sexual assault she never reported or held anyone responsible for.

After the event, in the dark of night, she was packing her Jeep for a well-deserved ten-day leave. The outdoor light did its best to illuminate the area. It was little help. But she saw a tall silhouette of a person lurking in the shadows.

Her panic instantly jerked her back nearly two decades earlier and dropped her into the middle of that earlier targeted assault as a young cadet. Claudia remembered the sounds, smells, and torturous pain.

She quickly threw the last bag in her Jeep and slammed the hatch.

The man slowly stepped out of the shadow the building cast and headed toward her.

The reply sped through her mind in fast-forward, giving her just enough time to decide.

There would be no repeat of former assault. If this was going to happen again, she was going down fighting.

"Oooh, I get a lady with brass," he said with a ghoulish smile, apparently noticing her collar bars. "A Lieutenant Colonel!"

Claudia's power-house punch bashed him in the face and split his nose wide open. Blood flew everywhere.

But her preemptive strike only slowed him for a second. The assailant returned fire, landing a hard blow to her face, knocking her out.

When she came to, she had a bloodied lip, blackened and swollen eye, and no recollection of anything after the knockout punch.

A quick physical inventory confirmed it had not been a repeat of the past. Her offense put him on defense, and he ran without doing further damage.

The injuries from his retaliation were worth every bit of temporary disfigurement.

What wasn't temporary was the flood of memories, fear, regret, humiliation, and anger that this close-call triggered.

The officer felt so alone. She had no one she trusted enough to confide in—except this one single friend.

He was the one person. The one she'd trust any secret with. If she asked—he'd take it to his grave.

She told him—and he promised.

"I don't ever want to talk about this again," she pleaded with him. "I'll figure out how to deal with it, but I'm done thinking about it."

"Okay, but when you get your bearings, please reach out to this place," he said as he handed her the business card. "I've heard about them for years. And you like horses. Why not give it a shot?"

Months passed but the nightmares and flashbacks didn't.

She called us, made an appointment, and we met her in our parking lot.

"Please let me say we're very sorry for what happened to you. It's unconscionable," the therapist said.

The officer interrupted, "I appreciate that, but it's done and over. I really don't want to go back."

This decorated veteran was a smart woman. She knew things don't go away just because we stop talking about them. If it were that easy, why was she here?

"Ma'am, can I be honest and forward with you?" I said, not waiting for permission. "In order for us to help you, you need to *let* us help you. That means allowing us to journey with you back far enough to disarm the demons that have a grip on you."

I paused for a short breath. "We've worked with hundreds of veterans, many with military sexual trauma. We know what it will take to free them. There's way more to it than just surviving the attack. You need to survive *surviving it*."

Her journey, like the others, would take a walk through the stages of grief, forgiving herself, forgiving others, and claiming the redemption God offers.

"Can we call you Claudia?" I asked. "By the time we're done, we'll be pretty good friends, so we might as well start now."

"Let's take a walk so we can introduce you to some horses," the therapist said. "Do you have any experience with these beautiful animals?"

"I had a horse when I was a teenager. He was a beautiful Palomino, so I called him Pal." Claudia smiled from ear to ear. "That horse saved my life. He saved me from a monstrous depression when my dad died. I was only thirteen years old."

"Sounds like a very special horse—and friend."

"What do you think about that Palomino over there?" I pointed to Maverick, our new boy.

"He's stunning. Can I meet him?"

All three of us walked up to Maverick. Without hesitation, the horse promptly turned and walked away.

"We haven't spent much time with him yet. He just finished a two-week quarantine period, so this is new to him," I explained.

"It's okay, I'm used to working for my progress, defending my territory, and putting up walls to keep the unwanted out. I assume that's what he's doing."

My goodness, a lot was said between those lines and behind those words.

I love this work. Even when the horse looks uncooperative — he's at work. Her description of Maverick was a carbon-copy of how she'd been hiding and surviving for years.

"Let's have you start by grooming Maverick." We'd had Maverick tied at the rail of the arena with a safety knot before Claudia started her first part of the equine therapy session.

She was meticulous, supporting the mane and tail as she combed, careful not to rip any hair out.

"He looks iridescent. Your brushing brought that out. Well done," I said.

The therapist said, "Time to take him for a walk. Start with the lead rope on for the first two or three laps, then remove it and see if he follows."

The horse's head bobbed with each step.

The veteran finished the third lap and stopped to remove the lead. As she did, the horse wandered off. Not following her at all. Not even looking at her—or for her.

"Catch up to the horse and see if he pays attention to you. See if he tries to connect," I said.

Maverick was strategic about staying away from Claudia. When she went right, he went left. He wasn't aggressive or threatening, just had no interest in connecting with this veteran.

"There must be something about me he doesn't like or respect. I know enough about horses to know that he won't follow me if he doesn't respect me," the veteran remarked.

"You're right. Could be many reasons," the therapist remarked. "What reasons can you think of?"

"He doesn't know me. He's in unfamiliar surroundings so he wants to explore. He doesn't know my reputation or how capable I am, so he doesn't know he should respect me," Claudia said, sharpening her tone.

When the officer's energy and attitude changed, so did Maverick's.

My therapy partner dug deeper. "You said Maverick may not like you for some reason. What made you say that?"

"I know plenty of people who don't like me because of my rank. Maybe they're jealous or something. Especially men," the female officer declared.

Then Claudia took us all by surprise. She threw her arms in the air, just missing Maverick's face, and began shouting. "Maybe this horse is the same!"

The horse took a step back with every forward step the veteran took.

"Are you one of those guys? One of those who think I don't deserve these stripes?"

Trying to emotionally ground her and help her return to the present, the therapist said, "I'll bet you do run into that. You're an impressive woman."

Even though the therapeutic temperature had risen, my partner knew to take advantage of a critical opening. "Do you ever run into people who have a strong reaction to you who don't even know you're a veteran or have rank?"

That question not only touched a nerve, it scorched it.

"Why do you ask that?" Claudia asked defensively.

"I'm gonna be honest with you," the therapist said. "It is true, many female survivors of military sexual trauma who didn't fight back suffered less physical harm. But the trade was they suffered much deeper emotional harm."

Maverick moved closer to the vet as the therapist continued.

"They say they're angry or even hate the assailant," the therapist continued. "But often the survivor is angrier at themselves than anyone else."

"That's crazy! Why would I be angry at myself for doing what kept me from getting beaten to a pulp? Maybe even killed? I don't hate myself because I didn't fight back!"

The officer turned toward the arena gate and said, "I'm done. It's amazing how you twist it so I'm the bad guy. I'm to blame."

My therapy partner tried to clarify. "Claudia, that's not what I said. The survivor is never to blame. *Never.* But when a traumatic event like this is so violating, so horrific, our psyche tries to protect us by scrambling our perceptions and feelings. It takes time to straighten it out."

The horse positioned himself between us and the vet like he was calling for a time-out. But his gallant gesture apparently went unnoticed by the officer.

Claudia's facial expression screamed defiance, but her body posture told us she *got it.*

The veteran pivoted to the horse, then to us, and said, "Like I said, I'm done for today. I'm not sure what I think anymore. I need time to sort through it."

There is no good or soft way of saying the things you must when trying to reframe events and reactions. It seems inhumane.

But leaving the officer stuck, reliving the event over-and-over would have also been inhumane.

When Claudia left the arena, Maverick stood at the gate facing the parking lot where the officer's car was parked. The horse stood at attention watching the veteran get in and drive off.

Even after the car was out of sight, Maverick still *stood post.*

It was the respectful thing to do.

Claudia missed her next session. The officer knew we'd be concerned, so she checked in by voice mail.

"Ladies, sorry I missed my session. I'm okay but I need more time to think. I talked to the long-time friend that sent me your way in the first place. He's a good man. Thanks."

Her friend wasn't just any old friend. He was an old boyfriend—more like a fiancé.

He loved her dearly, but she loved the Army more.

They stayed close friends. She trusted him.

The following week we brought Maverick into the arena, hoping Claudia would surprise us by showing up. She had only two more weeks before she was scheduled to leave.

My therapy partner and I headed to the mare pasture. There she was—sitting in Trinity's Grace Garden.

This sweet garden spot was carved from our 67-acres for times like this. The butterflies and beautiful flowers help lift the weight when someone or something is pressing down so hard you can hardly breath.

It's a place where God rests and invites us to rest with Him.

"Claudia," I said softly, "it's good to see you."

My partner stepped close to her and began, "I'm sorry if what I said upset you. I certainly didn't mean to. But sometimes—"

"I don't blame you. It was just hard to hear because I know it's true," the officer admitted.

I motioned for the women to follow me. "Let's continue this conversation in the arena. Maverick's waiting for us."

The gelding stood with his chest pressed against the arena gate. When we came around the corner, the horse opened up with a full-throated whinny.

"Claudia, looks like Maverick missed you. How about you see if he'll follow you today."

The horse could barely wait for her to open the gate. With no warm-up they both took off, side-by-side.

When she stopped, he stopped. If she reversed her pattern, Maverick didn't miss a beat. With every matching move, the officer showered the horse with praise and affection.

"It's so different from before. Instead of the horse following me because I demanded his respect, it felt like he followed me because he likes me," she said, smiling. "He likes and forgives me, because he senses I've begun liking and forgiving myself."

The officer grabbed a tissue from her pocket and wiped her eyes.

"And I forgive myself—for not fighting back. I used to think I was a coward for not fighting. But now I realize at *that* time, in *that* place, it was what I needed to do. I'm not to blame for the attack. And its time I stopped living like I was."

Maverick took off at a dead gallop around the arena, sand flying, his mane whipped by his speed, and his tail straight out.

He looked confident, fearless, and liberated, just like the horse wanted Claudia to feel.

No more hiding, no more shame, and no more anger.

A few months after Claudia left our area, we received a card from her. On the front was a beautiful Palomino horse running across a meadow.

Hi, Ladies,

I wanted to let you know I'm doing well and what I've grown to love. I'm working with an equine center on the East Coast that helps veterans like you do. I'm their veteran advocate for female survivors of military sexual trauma. I can't thank you enough for helping me get back to who I was. Who I so wanted to be again.

PS, I borrowed your idea of the Grace Garden and created one here. I really did feel God's presence and His grace there and wanted that for me and others here too.

Father, how sweet the sound when someone so lost, so broken, is found by You and lives seeking Your presence. You are our Shepherd who never loses even one sheep. We know Your name, we know Your voice, and we know Your heart, and You know ours.

Thank you. In Jesus' name we say, Amen.

Author Note

Grace is undeserved favor. It can't be earned—it's given freely.

"Through many dangers, toils and snares, I have already come; 'Tis grace hath brought me safe thus far and grace will lead me home." – John Newton

"Your worst days are never so bad that you are beyond the reach of God's grace. And your best days are never so good that you are beyond the need of God's grace." – Jerry Bridges

"God's grace is like a tsunami, and the only way to experience it is to allow the tidal wave to carry you to places you never thought you'd go." – Scott Wilson

"You are not too dirty for God to cleanse. You are not too broken for God to fix. You are not too far for God to reach. You are not too guilty for God to forgive. And you are not too worthless for God to love." – Unknown

Chapter Twelve
Welcome To My Hell

Some topics are tougher than others to talk about. Some are horrendous, and some are so barbaric, the tellers would rather die than tell them.

In the late 2000's, an out-of-state military organization asked us to create an Equine Assisted Therapy program to treat a population of veterans that, still to this day, are massively under-identified and underserved.

They sent us two brave and honorable souls that for more than two decades hid in the shadows, refusing to reveal the details or seek help for their military sexual trauma.

The US Department of Veterans Affairs reports 1 in 3 women answer "yes" to experiencing military sexual trauma.

But servicewomen weren't who we were asked to treat. An astounding one in fifty men report the same traumas. The Department of Defense statistics report thirty-two active duty male service members are sexually assaulted, harassed, or violated in some personal manner every single day.

Every day.

Female or male, this is as personal as it gets, blasting through the emotional pain scale. It's as personal as it possibly can get. Continuously haunted by guilt, shame, humiliation, betrayal, and desperation for those who survived but wish they hadn't.

Most servicemen, no matter the branch or era, identify as masculine, physically strong, and well able to fight off aggressors and defend themselves. The two veterans who came to our center couldn't have better aligned with this description.

I interviewed survivors of male military sexual trauma (MMST), asking what their deepest wound and biggest impact was on their life. Their answers tore me up and enraged me at the same time.

"This changed everything for me. It changed how I see myself, even changed who I am. I don't even feel like a man anymore. A man wouldn't have let this happen to him. I am nothing."

"I got nothing left except scars on the outside and rage on the inside. I don't trust anybody—never will again."

"I finally got the guts to tell my CO. I told him about the four attacks, hoping he'd make it stop. But instead, he said if I 'let it happen' more than once, I must have wanted it. I left his office knowing I couldn't go back to my unit. I refused to go through this again, so I decided I would end it my way. Then I'd be done with this hell I'm living. My only friend in this garbage pit talked me out of it. I wish he hadn't."

"My wife kept pushing and pushing, asking why I drank so much. I told her she didn't want to know, but she kept pushing. She promised nothing would change between us, so I finally told her. But after I did—after I told her about the attacks—she stood up, didn't say a word, turned her back, and walked away. She barely touches me anymore. It's been nearly fifteen years. I never should've told her."

James and John served until their dishonorable discharge. It was delivered without even a mention of gratitude, or the courtesy of a why. They knew it wasn't unsuitability, gross misconduct, or desertion. Both were decorated with commendation medals and ribbons. It was widely known their discharges came as a consequence of reporting to their Commanding Officers about the trauma of their multiple and violent sexual assaults.

These COs chose to blame them instead of listening to them. Chastise them rather than get them help for their recurring night terrors, insomnia, rage, and suicidal thoughts.

We walked into several pastures searching for two horses that would team up with these broken veterans, but none would come close. Usually, they're curious and eager to engage.

We had one more herd to try. When I saw James approach Chet, I cringed. This horse's reputation was cranky and unengaging. I could tell the vet was a soft-hearted man and I really had hoped he'd team up with a friendlier horse.

John, taking a less diplomatic approach, stomped into the neighboring pasture, demanding to work with Jojo, one of our playful minis. I'm not sure if this pint-sized pal knew what he was getting into, but he obliged.

I've said it a million times—everything means something. Why did the "tough guy" choose the small, unassuming horse, while the shy, soft spoken one chose a 1200-pound pushy sort?

We all gathered in the corner of the arena as I instructed the veterans to remove the leads and let the horses get acquainted.

Chet and Jojo aren't pasture mates, so the sniffing and kicking didn't surprise us. Nothing too serious, just negotiating who was alpha.

But things tore loose when James opened up, sharing some graphic details of his assaults. Jojo collected his 400-pounds of happy-go-lucky and charged Chet at Mach speed. This full-size quarter-horse always stands his ground. He's his own man, and nobody, I mean nobody, messes with him. But today was a wild flip-flop.

Jojo continued his rant, relentlessly pursuing Chet, with mouth wide open, and baring his teeth. Rearing and screaming, the mini tried to mount the 15.2 gelding, over and over.

Stunned, my partner whispered her concern about Jojo's behavior, and suggested I pull him from the session.

For a split second I agreed, then reluctantly replied, "Let's let it play out. We'll count on the horses to tell the story they need to, so we can better understand what these guys are dealing with."

By this time, we'd worked with veterans for almost ten years, and had conducted hundreds of sessions. But we'd never, ever seen anything like this. It was like Dr. Jekyll and Mr. Hyde. Our horses just don't behave like this.

The veterans stood with their backs against the arena wall, watching this battle play out in front of them.

I heard James whisper, "He was so much smaller than me, like Jojo. I should've been able to push him away. But I couldn't. I don't know why."

James' whispers continued. "I couldn't outrun them. They cornered me like Jojo is trying to do to Chet. There was nowhere to go, no sense in fighting. It was going to happen no matter what."

We asked, "You said *them*? Was there more than one who attacked you?"

"Yeah, there were four who took turns." James sobbed.

Horses are so sensitive. They tap into the energy of their surroundings, positive or negative. It was clear the horses wanted no part of the vile flashbacks. They sought refuge in the farthest corner. Normally I'd look for ways to reengage the horses, but honestly, they needed the break.

We were only halfway through our fifty-minute session when I said. "Hey guys, thanks for your honesty and good work today, but let's take this one step at a time. I know it's hard on you, so we're going to stop for today. We'll pick it up again next week."

James looked relieved, while John looked disappointed. Like I was the MMA referee who prematurely called the fight.

After they left, we debriefed, starting with a prayer of cleansing. We needed to rid our space from the darkness these guys unintentionally carried in.

What we heard from them and the reaction of the horses was impossible to shake. Both vets admitted they'd never told anyone what they'd told us. This was by far the most intense and unsettling session we've ever conducted.

The following week, we brought the horses into the arena prior to our veterans joining us. We wanted to take the horses' emotional temperature so we didn't have a repeat of the previous week.

But the animals acted as if nothing happened. Like it was a figment of our imagination. Much like how these veterans were made to feel. If no one believed them, then it didn't happen.

Once they arrived, we had James and John join us in the arena, greet their horse, and lead them around for a few laps.

"Hey guys, bring your horses over to the middle. Let's try something different. I want you to drop the lead to the ground, place your hands on the side of your horse, and take three deep breaths. That's it. Good work. Now, close your eyes and just stand quietly."

John emphatically refused, "There's no way I'm going to close my eyes. That's when all the visions come back. Oh, heck no!" His words were peppered with profanity. Nothing we hadn't heard before. He certainly made himself clear – he would not be closing his eyes.

James followed the instructions to the letter. After he wiggled his feet deep into a stable stance, he closed his eyes hard, creating deep creases across his face.

We could see the stress was still gripping both of them, so we tried another technique to break its grip.

"Take two steps back from your horse, inhale a big, full breath, hold it for a moment, then exhale hard while you do a full body shake. Yup, from your head to your feet, shake it out! Now try the exercise again."

BAM, there it was. James stepped back in, methodically placed his hands on Chet's sides, took his three big breaths, and closed his eyes. Within moments, James looked like he was transported to a different place and time. A smile replaced the grimace, and his breathing slowed and softened.

John fidgeted the entire time. Shuffling his feet, mumbling to himself, looking put out, and refusing to do most everything.

I disregarded John's displeasure and rolled on, "Tell us what that was like for you."

"It was stupid. What did you expect would happen? It would be some magic bullet, some absurd reversal of everything we experienced? Some trick of erasing our memories?" John spit back.

I didn't take the bait. I knew this veteran was more interested in picking a fight than finding a path to recovery.

I calmly responded, "Quite the contrary. Often when someone rests their hands on the horse, the two—horse and human—relax together. The horse tends to ground and calm the client. They sometimes even begin breathing in the same cadence."

James broke in, "That's what happened to me. Chet and I were, well, like...together. I really liked it. Chet makes me feel calm. I haven't felt that in a long time."

Our horses pick up what people put out. Chet could tell James wanted to reconcile his feelings, tame his demons, and become whole again. It was easy to see all John wanted was to go nose-to-nose in the arena with his monsters of shame and humiliation.

"Now it's time for our first test. Take the leads off your horse, turn your back, and start walking away from them. Let's see what your horse does."

Chet, the formerly crabby gelding, surprisingly never hesitated. Off he went right on James's heels. On the second lap, the horse actually trotted to catch up to James, so they could walk shoulder-to-shoulder. The horse matched the veteran's pace peacefully, and perfectly.

John left his horse in the dust. Seemed he took off to prove there was no connection, no way this horse would follow him and moreover, the veteran didn't even want him to. Seems like John wanted to feed his preconceived notion that if he did try, and the horse refused, that would be just one more denial, rejection, and failure. Maybe even heartbreak.

Sometimes we bring chairs into the arena to sit and watch what happens when the horses are free to roam and don't think we're watching them.

They both circled us a few times, then Chet began to weave through us, while Jojo chose to stay on the edge. Our plan was to spend the rest of our session processing the "you lead; I'll follow" activity.

But apparently Chet didn't get the memo. He parked right in front of James, lowering his head into the vet's lap. I know this horse very well. I mean very well, and he hates having his head messed with. If you even try, he'll pull away and hoist it up beyond your reach. We learned fast that these sessions, with these guys, would be like no other.

Weeks went by and John's demeanor changed little. No matter the exercise, the activity, even when we pulled the best "trick" out of our hat, not much moved him. The menacing memories had such a grip on him, and after reliving them for over twenty years, the rut in his psyche was miles deep.

That's what we fight here. It's not just the residual memories, it's what our minds do or don't do with them.

We moved to the covered round pen—my favorite venue. Sixty feet in diameter, one gate, with six-foot-high open rails. You wouldn't think a shape would make such a change, but I've seen it shift and change everything. That's why I'm so fond of it.

Jojo and John finally found their groove. I guess both horse and human were calmed by the round, never-ending feel of support. There were no corners for a perpetrator to hide, and no blinds spots. It might just be the magic bullet John insisted didn't exist. But we knew he secretly was desperate for it to be so.

My partner took James to a different space while I worked with John.

"Are you ready to try this again?" I smiled and asked.

"The breathing and the hands thing? Dang, I feel like a healing monk...laying hands on." He scoffed, but with a smile this time.

"Yup, the whole nine yards," I answered. "Remember to start with leading him for a few laps like you did in the main arena."

Lap after lap, John kept quiet. I didn't want to interrupt if some invisible transformation was in process. Then, without my asking, the vet stopped his horse in the middle, dropped the lead to the ground, and began to walk away from him, not even turning to see if the horse was following.

He got about ten feet from him, and Jojo popped his head up, then trotted straight to John. The vet whipped around and dropped to his knees to greet his new 38-inch-tall friend.

Barely able to hide my excitement, I straightened and asked, "So John, how did that feel? How was it different than how you felt in the other space?"

I figured the veteran would take his time answering, and even maybe throw me some sarcasm to buffer the amazing happening, but nope. Not this time.

He smiled, not once taking his hands off Jojo and said, "Never experienced anything like that. I'm not sure how it makes me feel. I guess it makes me feel like...maybe he likes me, just for me. He didn't judge me like everyone else does who knows what happened. He makes me feel kinda special and accepted. I forgot what that was like. I haven't felt that in over twenty-five years. I guess there was a little magic to this," he said as he raised his eyebrows.

"Nah," I said. "That's God making sure you don't miss the chance to open your heart and feel it again. He's in the business of changing lives, and making transformations. I believe He's on to you."

Father, you truly are our Redeemer and Savior. You save us from the demons who chase us and try to devour us. Thank You for touching these two remarkable men. May You replace the hurt in their hearts with the peace that only You can provide. In Jesus' name we pray.

Author Note

Military Sexual Trauma, no matter if male or female, is often kept a secret to the survivor's detriment. It often contributes to the twenty-two veterans we lose every day to suicide. If this has happened to you, please know you are not alone. There's help out there. Please check into the resources below. God bless you.

Some resources that may help:
- maketheconnection.net
- mentalhealth.va.gov – "Men overcoming Military Sexual Trauma"
- https://www.dav.org "Military Sexual Trauma – MST"
- https://www.woodslawyers.com "Male victims of Military Sexual Trauma (MST) Can Get VA Disability for PTSD."
- www.nctrc.org – Military Sexual Trauma Resource List
- www.safehelpline.org - Military Men – Anonymous help
- Sexual Hotline 877-995-5247

Chapter Thirteen
Living My Tornado

Jason filled our conference room door with his 6'4", 280-pound frame. He was a US Army veteran for more than half his life. Other than his size, the thing I noticed was his eyes. They were menacing, and void of life. Something I hadn't seen for over fifty years. They sent chills up my spine, a trigger through my psyche, flashing me back to a 9-year-old doting daughter, on the floor in a choke hold, staring into my father's eyes—a career US Army veteran with PTSD.

I was instantly torn between the fear of accidentally triggering Jason, as I did my dad, and the deep compassion I felt for this vet.

Our standard welcome and introduction was swirling around in my head but refusing to come out of my mouth. My therapy partner chimed in, "Hi Jason, we're glad you're here." She started strong and straightforward. "What's going on that brought you here today?"

He said, "The chaos, the carnage that surrounds me—the tornado." He fixed his gaze on us and continued. "Are you afraid of me? Do you think I'll hurt you?"

We quickly answered, "No, of course not." But I secretly wondered, *if he thought to ask, should we be?*

His growing resentment was palpable as we flipped through introductory questions. We're used to veterans coming in angry and feeling judged. They feel like they're being watched, analyzed, and studied. Like caged animals. Even though our methods are far different than the Veterans Administration, or traditional therapy, he didn't know that yet. We could tell Jason was trying to hold back, but the tornado was about to touch down.

We learned long ago that the issues our veterans hide aren't all a result of their military experiences. Abuse, trauma, neglect, and unresolved relational conflicts caused havoc well before they ever enlisted. Add those ingredients to *combat* trauma, death, guilt, and shame, and you'll have a very unsavory dish to pass.

It was obvious Jason and his wife were in the middle of a vicious game of Gottcha. *You did this… so I did that! If you wouldn't have… I wouldn't have.* On and on it went, until we intervened and insisted we go for a herd walk. The therapist took the wife; I took Jason.

We intentionally headed in two different directions, hoping that each one's true nature would be revealed.

Jason's comment came out of nowhere. "How can I be forgiven when I spent all week teaching my unit how to kill? What am I supposed to do? Go to church on Sunday and ask forgiveness? I don't think so. God doesn't work that way."

Jason and I walked through the pastures, meeting each horse to see if any showed interest in working with him.

He spied Hugo, way across the landscape. The horse was a scrawny, small-framed gelding that was covered with scrapes, cuts, and scars. Some so deep no hair would have the courage to ever grow back. Before Trinity, the horse had been kept in a herd where he was relentlessly bullied. The last to eat, and the last to drink. He suffered from raging PTSD. Even after arriving at Trinity, Hugo spent all his time alone, far from his herd mates.

"Who's he?" the veteran pointed.

"He's fresh on the ranch. One of our few rescues," I replied.

I've been accused more than once of being a softy, but all I could imagine was the horse wondering what'd he ever done to deserve this?

Hugo was having a tough time adjusting to the hustle and bustle of Trinity. He was losing the weight he came with, and his injuries needed attention. He was terrified of his new surroundings, the other horses, and us.

We weren't about to play the "name that horse" game with the veteran, so when Jason asked, I answered. "That's Hugo."

"Who beat him up?"

"Don't know, but he barely eats, and we've never seen him drink. Soon it'll become a big deal if that doesn't change. We've tried everything. Nothing's worked so far. He won't let any of us near him."

Jason mumbled, "He reminds me of the people who say they're afraid to be around me. My friends, family, even my wife. They're scared I'm going to freak out and hurt them. Maybe worse."

I couldn't disagree.

"Can we go in with him?" he asked.

"Of course, but I have no idea how he'll react."

"It's okay. I'm used to that."

The veteran went on, "I don't mean to scare people. But when I drink, I drink to get passed-out drunk, so I don't have to fight through the nightmares night after night. My wife has seen me at my worst, my lowest point. My meanest. No wonder she's so afraid of me."

As we entered Hugo's pasture, the horse was nowhere to be found. We scoured the entire acreage, and nearly gave up, thinking maybe someone moved him to a private turnout after we saw him. We made one final pass, going behind the far shelter, and there he was, lying flat out.

I gasped, "Oh no, I was afraid this might happen.

Sometimes when a horse won't drink, it helps to put a bit of salt in a few scoops of applesauce and syringe it into the side of their mouth. The applesauce makes it palatable, and the salt makes them thirsty. But because he wouldn't let us near him, we went to plan B. Adding molasses and unflavored electrolytes to his bucket of water might tempt him to drink. We prayed it would, but looking at him, I guessed not.

The clock was ticking. We know a horse can go without food for almost a month, but only 48 hours without water before all sorts of bad things start to happen. If he hasn't taken in significant water within four days, he'll be gone.

Jason ran up to him, dropped to his knees, and huffed, "What can we do? How can we help him?"

I grabbed my cell, called my staff partner, told her what happened, and asked her to let Jason's wife know the session was over. We knew they drove separately, so that meant one less person to manage during a crisis.

The veteran heard and looked at me with wide eyes filled with tears. His eyes... changed. They weren't the lifeless, coal-colored eyes I saw in the office. They were soft blue, full of spirit, compassion, even love!

I regretted having to say, "Jason, I can't let you stay. Not with this happening." I told him he needed to leave, so I could tend to the horse.

"I'm not leaving. Maybe I can help. Can I please stay? I'll do anything."

I silently weighed the pros and cons.

"Alright, but if you're staying, you're one of us. We have to get him up, or this'll go south real fast. He looks weak, so we'll have to help him."

Jason didn't look confident, but determined. We had to move quickly.

"On the count of three, let's try to help him up. One, two, three, GO!"

No luck. Hugo had nothing to give.

"Let's try again," I yelled. "One, two, three, GO! Harder, harder!"

We tried rocking him, coming from different angles, sweet-talking him, even being harsh and hollering, but nothing worked. We needed him up, now!

"Jason, while I call Doc, stay by the horse's head. Talk to him and rub his neck. Tell him he'll be okay."

The veteran was on a mission. He took on an entirely different persona. Jason was calm, compassionate, and began to comfort Hugo.

"Hey buddy, I know we haven't really met yet, but you can trust me. I never let any of my uni's down, and I won't let you down either."

To add to the surprises of the day, the veteran started unloading his "baggage" on Hugo, spilling his regrets and shame. No doubt a load he'd been carrying for a very long time.

"I feel terrible about how I treat my wife. I screwed up my other marriages, and I sure don't wanna trash this one." He spoke in a steady, warm, and caring tone. He only took his hands off Hugo's neck long enough to wipe his tears.

"Truth be told, I'm as scared as you are. But at least you have the courage to show it, and not run from it, like me. I'm scared that if I let my anger out, the tornado I'm trying so hard to keep under control might...really hurt someone. Maybe even my wife. So when I push her away, I'm trying to protect her. When I drink until I pass out, at least I won't hurt her. It's my tornado that keeps spinning around me, in my mind, and keeps picking up things in its path, lambasting everything and everyone.

Even though twenty feet separated us when I stepped away to make the call for help, I heard everything. Every confession, every sad comment, and every regret. That's what I call a therapeutic moment!

Then I heard Doc's voice asking, "What we got?"

"Doc, it's Trinity. Remember the little gelding we rescued a few weeks ago? Well, it happened. He went down and there's no getting him up. He's really dehydrated. We need your help quickly! This is the little guy with no trust."

Rejoining Jason and Hugo, I saw fear plastered across the veteran's face, like he'd done something wrong. Hugo was standing!

"How'd you get him up?"

"He just stood up by himself. I tried to keep him calm and still, like you said, but he got really anxious, and popped up. But he won't let me near him again. If I try, he staggers off. He's so weak and wobbly."

"It's okay, Jason. You did good. Horses are like us. They'll do things that'll harm them when they're scared. They'll even refuse help when they know they need it. I just hope he'll let us save him."

Those words didn't fall on deaf ears. The veteran sat back on his rump for a moment, and then said, "I can sure relate to that. That's been my story since I got out."

By now my equine manager was in the dirt next to me, and whispered, "I'll take over so you can get your client out of here. He doesn't need to see Doc's work."

It's often unsettling to watch veterinarians at work. They do what they have to in order to save the animal. Doesn't mean it's pretty.

I whispered to my manager, "Normally, I'd never let something roll out like this, but the veteran is smack in the middle of an epiphany. And honestly, if I tell him to leave, all that would crumble. I'm sure he'd never come back, and that would be the ultimate tragedy."

She said, "Yes ma'am, you're the boss."

We needed to get close to Hugo before Doc arrived. I slowly walked towards the horse, talking in a calm tone. At first Hugo looked like he'd allow it, but quickly fear took over, and he barely caught his fall as he tried to get away.

"I need one of you to meet Doc in the driveway, so he knows where we are."

Trinity's size and Hugo's desperate need meant we couldn't afford the wasted time if Doc needed to search for us.

"I'll do it!" Jason said. "What does he drive?"

"A big red pickup."

"I'm on it!" Jason shouted over his back and took off like a bullet running through the pasture. He reached the barn at full speed, but I lost sight of him as he headed down the drive.

Before we knew it, we saw the veteran and veterinarian pull through the gate and park right beside us.

Doc asked, "Who's got the best chance getting close to this boy? We'll have only one try at this, then any amount of trust'll be gone."

I looked at my manager, she looked at me, and we both looked at Jason.

"Jason's our best chance, Doc."

I quickly offered up a prayer while the veteran walked towards the horse.

"Father, please give Jason, your son and servant, the heart he needs to gain Hugo's trust. You know what needs to happen here. You know what it'll take to save this horse. Hugo will help lots of people who struggle with fear, but he needs to survive to serve. We're all scared and need your calm and peace. We ask everything in your name Jesus, Amen."

Jason spoke slowly and quietly to Hugo, but we heard every word. "You heard that prayer, didn't you, boy. That was for both you and me. Me the old servant, and you the new one. Nobody's ever prayed for me before. How about you? Let's do this friend. Nice and easy."

He did it! The halter was on, and the process of getting Hugo the fluids he needed had begun.

Jason insisted on staying right next to him. As he rubbed Hugo's neck, he told the horse what a good boy he was, and kept the focus on him as the fluid flowed in.

After we were able to take a breath, we knew this day would undoubtedly change both the horse and the veteran. God is so good. He allowed us to witness the trust explode between the two. Better yet, to see Jason and Hugo become the combat comrades they were destined to be.

That day—that crisis and that blessing—was cathartic for Jason. It changed him in dramatic ways—instantly.

Usually the evolution takes weeks, even months before we see a hint of it. But not for this veteran, and not with this horse.

Jason was different from that day forward. Sure, he still had his windstorms now and then, but never again did he have his dreaded tornadoes.

We continued to see the veteran weekly for almost a year. His marriage not only survived but thrived after this event. Jason's new ability to open his heart, share his feelings and fears was the change needed to start his journey of rebuilding his relationships. Best of all, he was committed to growing his relationship with Jesus, and receiving the forgiveness and redemption he so needed.

Father, You are our redeemer, forgiver, savior, and friend. You meet us in our time of crisis and need. Thank You for never leaving us behind. For never abandoning us, no matter how resistant we are. You are our creator of new beginnings, and of fresh starts. Amen, amen.

Author Note

Trust is a fragile commodity. I use that term because I believe a "commodity" is something we trade. Maybe we think of dollars in trade for a cup of coffee. Twenty dollars for an hour of time. A commodity is a traded value.

My dad always told me he'd trust me until I gave him a reason not to. Trust is an essential commodity in any relationship. Hard to give, easy to retract.

In our world, the horse world, trust is the first and sometimes only commodity that matters when you're working with horses and veterans with PTSD. Trust for both is everything. When it's broken, it's nearly impossible to mend. But the nature of our work practices the art of rebuilding trust. Splinting the trust-fractured heart takes precision and time. Often, lots of time.

With our clients, and I believe with all people, trust begins with a connection. There's something that draws us to another. If we nurture and manage that well, it progresses to a relationship. Then, perhaps to a valued relationship, even a deep friendship. After enough time and devotion to that relationship, a bond of trust is born. With more time and attention, that trust becomes durable, resilient, and something worthy of protecting.

Without it, we have nothing to barter, nothing to give, nothing that has value to build a foundation on. If something threatens that trust while the relationship is growing, one of us stands back and assesses whether the other was trustworthy at all.

Even we humans need a leader, but not just any leader. One we can trust when all the wheels fall off. When we need protection, forgiveness, and to be embraced. There is no human who can fill those shoes. No person, group, coalition, political or social party that we can trust the way we can trust our Father, His Son, and the Holy Spirit.

In Jeremiah 29:11, Jesus talks about the plans He has for us. The plans for good, not to destroy us. The ones that pave a way for our future, our purpose, and to live in harmony with Him. That's the kind of leader we need.

In John 14:2 Jesus promises that He's gone ahead of us, to save space in His Father's home. He tells us there's room enough for us all! That's our kind of trustworthy leader.

Do you struggle with trust? Has your past trained you to never trust anyone? If so, you might want to tune in to a new leader. A strong, righteous leader. One who knows you, loves you, forgives you, and leads you to His promised land. That's the leader I follow. How about you?

Chapter Fourteen
At the Hands of the Potter

His sleeveless punk rock shirt proudly displayed his bulging biceps and the maze of single-colored tattoos covering both arms from wrist to shoulder. Screaming in defiance was the small, delicate cross imprinted on the topside of his right hand.

I confess if his goal was to intimidate — mission accomplished.

But we'd never let him know it.

"So where's this horse I'm supposed to break?" veteran parolee #0405 demanded.

Are you kidding? Who told this brute he was here to break one of our horses? I struggled to calm my voice, then said, "Sounds like you got some bad information. Breaking horses isn't part of our program. We partner with them to help vets get a fresh start."

The veteran shouted, "That's not what I signed up for."

"Your file says you're here on a court order to complete our eight-week equine-assisted therapy program for newly released veterans."

The moment I uttered the word "therapy," I knew things would go to the next level of bad.

"I don't need no therapy! I didn't consent to this!" he fired off.

"I'm sure consent doesn't enter into it. The court-ordered part takes care of that," I said, setting my boundaries.

The document didn't say what he was charged with or convicted of. What bad choice did this veteran make to earn him ten years in a medium-security prison?

My therapy partner and I knew the risks and rules.

No weapons, drugs, alcohol, personal contact with us or others here, or disrespect.

Not sure how we'd measure that last one.

"Since you're here, let's get started. What do you want us to call you?" I asked in a monotone voice.

"05," he replied, matching my tone, "Call me that."

It took a second — but then it clicked. 05 was short for #0405.

There was no need for our standard herd walk since we'd already picked his horse.

We chose Esther. This mare was the pushiest, most arrogant, stand-your-ground horse we had. She's an 18-hand powerhouse. Nearly a ton of tough and crank, with only a sliver of patience.

In the Bible, she'd be Queen Esther, but at Trinity, she's earned the title Esther the Beast.

There's a steep learning curve when working with veteran inmates or recently released parolees. You can tap into those who've either practiced it or researched and tested their theories. Trinity's been blessed to have both.

Some people, groups, and legislators don't want to bother with veteran felons. They believe they've earned where they've landed.

We see it differently.

There's no disputing that some of these veteran inmates have done monstrous things — but that doesn't make them monsters.

They deserve a chance for rehabilitation. A chance to reshape, redefine, and repurpose their lives.

Everyone deserves redemption.

Our many years of serving veterans reveal an often tragic chain of events that causes a matching tragic chain of consequences.

The year 2017 marked our fourth appearance before the WI State Senate and Committee on Veterans Affairs. I testified to help win support for our state's veterans struggling with PTSD through the addition of a grant fund to Wisconsin's annual budget.

"It starts when a veteran's military experience causes trauma. This trauma leads to a physical, emotional, or spiritual injury that produces PTSD," I said, making my point. "Many of these veterans avoid or refuse treatment because they fear losing rank, status, or their military benefits. So instead, they choose to live, fight, and often lose the battle to their undiagnosed, untreated mental health issues."

You could hear a pin drop in the chamber.

I continued, "They desperately try to 'tame their demons' by self-medicating and over-using drugs and alcohol. Their impaired judgment, impulsive behavior, and rebellious reactions often result in a violent clash with Law Enforcement."

My long-time friend, co-author of this piece of legislation and Chairman of the committee signaled his full support.

"Individuals who are impaired by substances and without the emotional skills to control their behavior leave Law Enforcement no choice but to arrest them. The DA brings charges, and our courts convict, sentence, and incarcerate," I detailed. "Will you help us break this cycle?"

With "05," we met at the round pen to start our first equine session. The veteran stood outside the pen, looking as *bad* as he possibly could.

"05, come on in and meet this horse. Her name is Esther."

The vet entered slowly, looking from side to side as if someone might ambush him. He jumped a good two feet when the gate closed behind him with a slam.

He rushed to regain his cool, refusing to look flustered or fearful. He used his cool as one of his prison weapons, along with his language, posture, how he walked, and how he talked. It all creates the necessary facade to keep others away, to keep him as safe as possible in a place like that.

"She don't look so tough!" 05 barked after he stole a peek to see her gender.

The veteran strutted towards her with his chest pushed out past comfort, his lower lip jutting out, and his arms raised high above his head. Of course, he used intimidation as his strategy. But he'd never met this mare. She *is* intimidation.

The veteran turned to face us, spewing, "I'm not afraid of her. This'll be easy."

When he turned back, Esther towered over him. The horse pounded his face with her hot moist breath, staring him in the eyes and leaning against his chest to model real intimidation.

"What was that you were saying, 05?"

The veteran jumped back, swearing under his breath. He turned towards us and threw us an over-exaggerated shoulder shrug like we were obligated to smooth the introduction for him.

He gathered his swagger and headed back for round two.

Esther didn't give an inch. She's the kind of lady that, if approached respectfully, a negotiation could be found, but it would have to be on her terms.

For someone who didn't know the process, it might have looked like Groundhog Day at the OK Corral as weeks passed without progress.

We knew it was a test. There's always a test.

It's *will* versus *want*. The will to remain rough, hardened, and unchanged versus the inescapable primal longing to be accepted, included, and even loved.

We'd hit the halfway mark on our eight-week series, and I was feeling the pressure to show progress. A little crack in the armor to tell us we were making a dent. Often it's a change in language or a more congenial and cooperative attitude. Anything that hints of a change on our side of the slate. But it was a no-go with this veteran. Not this parolee.

Before 05 arrived that next session, I anxiously approached my therapy partner.

"How about we push on this a bit? Pull out one of our tried-and-tested activities and open this puppy up?"

"And miss all the fun?" The therapist smiled. "Miss what God's got in store for this young man? You know how the Master Potter works... kneading, pushing, and forcing all the air out of the pores until there's no resemblance to the former."

I saw the look in my therapy partner's eyes. She was on a roll.

"It lies shapeless on the wheel until with love — deep love and compassion—God smooths all the rough edges and reshapes it. He returns it to its original image and purpose. That's a transfiguration of a lifetime. No, ma'am, let's wait."

She was right. She was usually right. The Spirit uses times like these to remind us — remind me — that impatience is really an issue of trust. The desire to control outcomes is more about ego than deliverance. It reminds us that this life is about reshaping and preparing us for the next.

Week five started the same, with 05 pushing and retreating. Esther appeared bored with the weekly replay, so she launched her own "seek and ye shall find" lesson.

The horse surprised the veteran by approaching him and assertively brushing against his arm with her face. She repeated this two, three, four times.

"What's she doing? Why's she pushing me like that? She wanna fight? She gonna bite?" The veteran nervously asked.

My therapy partner calmly asked, "What about her behavior seems threatening or aggressive to you?"

"She's touching me! Isn't that a big enough clue?"

"You tell us. What else could it be?" she asked.

Esther began brushing his arm again. She stopped, turned, and walked away. The horse stood parallel to the pen rails. Not facing him — that's too inviting. Not rear view — that'd invite easy criticism.

She stood in neutrality. Ready to pivot either way.

Choices, choices. Would he surrender or stay a prison-made man?

The parolee wasn't ready to commit. So the vet began his own game of sorts.

He first faced Esther, making sure she saw him fully, then quickly turned away. Then he did it again and again. The horse shook her head as if his warped game of peek-a-boo was making her head spin.

Esther looked like she might have even been a bit embarrassed for him, so she turned tail and walked to the furthest side of the pen. 05 was clearly frustrated, so he gladly followed us out of the round pen to end the session. He started following us to the parking lot but stopped only after walking a few feet from the pen gate. He turned and faced the horse.

We noticed but decided to give him some space.

05 walked back to the gate, draped his arms over the top of it, and leaned against it. Not saying a word or moving an inch. He just stood there and stared at Esther.

The horse matched his stare and stance.

"I don't know what you want from me," 05 whispered. "Maybe we're way too much alike. You're stubborn like me. You've got a nasty attitude like me, and you're pushy like me. Maybe we can strike a truce or something, huh?" he offered.

Esther doesn't fold that easily. She'll make him work a bit more to earn a compromise.

Our seventh week started with 05 chanting, "It's a fresh-start Friday. It's a fresh-start Friday."

I looked puzzled, so he piped up, "Yes, ma'am, you said this program gives fresh starts, right?"

"Yup, that's right."

"Okay then, tell me why Esther rubbed on me that way? She didn't seem mad. Maybe it was a game or it was as if she liked it."

What happened to this man between the time he left us and returned?

My mind was swimming in muddy water.

First, he called me ma'am. Then, he called Esther by her name. And now he was asking us questions instead of slamming us with bully-like statements. Can you spell progress?

"Well, 05..." I started.

"Stop!" the veteran interrupted. "My name is Daniel. Will you ladies please call me Daniel?"

Boy, when God says it's go-time, He really pulls out all the stops.

I started again, "Horses are naturally affectionate animals — even Esther. Rubbing your arm might be her way of making a connection, Daniel."

"Really, even after I called her those names and treated her like I did? She'd still wanna be my friend?"

"I don't know about that. But I do know God wired horses to be full of forgiveness for our mistakes and full of faith in us to do better," I said. "And as for the friendship — that's a conversation you'll have to have with Esther."

"Ha, a conversation with her? Horses can't talk...can they?" The veteran cocked his head in confusion.

I turned away, leaving the question hanging in mid-air.

Daniel entered the round pen, slowly walked up to the horse, and said, "Hi, Esther, I'm Daniel. I'm very glad to meet you. I want to apologize for all the bad words I've been using and how I've treated you. I'd like to be your friend if you'd like to be mine."

It was as if we stepped into Hitchcock's "Twilight Zone," only a reverse version.

My therapy partner and I slowly tip-toed backward to give Daniel more privacy. When we met the rail behind us, we quietly shared a smile and a wink of celebration.

Now here we were, week eight — our last with Daniel. We'd been dreading this day.

Esther waited for the vet to cross the driveway.

"I come bearing gifts for my lady!" Daniel said with a Shakespearean flair.

From his pocket, he pulled a bag of apples that were cut into bite-sized pieces.

The vet straightened up, put on his most professor-like persona, and reported, "I read up on horse treats last night, and it said horses love apples, but they can choke on them if you don't cut them up. So I did."

He softened and asked, "Do you think it'd be okay if our last session was just Esther and me? I want us to be together just as friends, not working on anything. She's already taught me so much."

I couldn't miss the cross-over. That's exactly what God wants from us. Just our desire to be with Him. No agenda. Just friends.

"You bet," I said, grinning from ear to ear, "We'll be over by the tree if you need anything."

Time was up. Daniel and Esther said their final goodbye with what could only be described as a long, loving hug.

Daniel's head was buried in the horse's mane with his arms wrapped around her neck. And Esther curled her mammoth head and neck around Daniel's torso, holding him firmly but ever-so-gently.

As we walked the veteran to his car, Esther stood at the gate, nickering an extra farewell.

I finally ask, "Daniel, since we met, I've wanted to ask you about the cross on your hand. What's the story?"

"My mom loved Jesus. She passed while I was in prison, but she always told me Jesus loved me too — and that He'd never leave me. So I got this to honor her belief. Mom was so sure God would guide me no matter what happened in my life."

We saw how Daniel was affected by telling us about his mom.

"It's been a long haul with my PTSD and all that happened because of it, but I'm starting to believe her. How could I not? He's the one who guided me here."

I reached to give Daniel a goodbye hug. He cracked a huge smile and said, "Looks like we're about to break a rule, huh?"

"You've earned it," I said. "Well done."

Those eight weeks not only changed Daniel, they changed us too. That's how God works.

Daniel spent ten years in the lion's den of prison. And when released, God rescued him from himself. Through the vet's work with Esther, God smoothed his rough edges and returned him to the shape and purpose he was created for.

It was a holy transfiguration.

...and when God finished, He turned to admire His work and smiled. On the Master Potter's wheel rested a new radiant creation. It was a heart — Daniel's new reborn heart.

Father, You are the Master Potter. You are the reshaper, rebuilder, and renewer of our hearts and lives. Thank You for loving us so much that You refuse to leave us as we are. Thank You for Your guidance and forever offer of redemption. Amen, amen.

Author Note
Redemption vs. Forgiveness.

I confess these two terms feel so intertwined they may seem interchangeable. But they aren't.

For me, it looks like a two-sided coin. One side reads *our debt problem*, the other, *our sin problem*.

It's all about sin and love.

Our debt problem is our sin. "The wages of sin is death." So if we sin, we die — not physically, but spiritually. God loves us too much to leave it there, so He took on all our sins, took on our death sentence, and traded our death for His. We are redeemed.

Our forgiveness problem is our sin. We sin daily. Sin creates a darkness that separates us from God. God loves us too much to leave it there, so He grants us forgiveness when we ask for it.

Because God loves us — He redeems us.

Because God loves us — He forgives us.

Chapter Fifteen
Free Will

God is the perfect planner, and planter. Long before our birth, God planned every day of our lives. Our Father is omnipotent, omniscient, and omnipresent. All powerful. All knowing. All present.

Yet the scriptures don't dodge the fact that our lives will be dotted with triumph, trial, and even some tragedy. It's why He planted seeds of purpose and passion to help reinforce our resolve.

"Surely, as I have planned, so it will be, and as I have purposed, so it will happen," reads Isaiah 14:24 NIV.

Just when we think our guardrails are secure, He seems to throw caution to the wind, and gives us endless options. In Deuteronomy 30:19 God speaks of giving mankind the gift of free will – the gift of choice.

What? Freedom to do whatever we want? That's a risky move. Would you give your children that range of freedom? Not me.

As a young mother, I cleverly controlled the options given to our boys by only offering safe, Mom-approved choices. It worked like a charm. It tamed my worries, while giving them the illusion of say-so when I insisted, "Make good choices."

But "hands-off," "let go of the reins," free will would be terrifying as a parent.

Still our Father insists we have the freedom to invite Him as our Savior – or be indifferent to Him. To follow Him – or be unfaithful to Him.

He insists if we choose Him, it must be from desire, not demand.

However, immunity was never part of God's freedom promise. This non-negotiable fact has caused the endless rivalry between choice and consequence.

Our choices are easily influenced by people, moods, and situations. Yet their consequences, by definition, are impartial – they have no opinion. They are simply the result of our choices.

In fact, research reports humans make an astounding 35,000 "remotely conscious" choices every day, oblivious to the correlation between what was done, and what happened because of it.

In stark contrast, horses are "rigorously conscious" creatures. It's how they stay safe, well fed, surrounded by companions, and content.

Of all God's creatures, we chose horses to partner with at Trinity. They're some of His most beautiful and inspired work, and we're not too snooty to say they double as our teachers.

Authenticity, transparency, and honesty come naturally to them. Not so much for us. It runs cross-grain to our insatiable drive to control and deflect.

I've spent nearly six decades being schooled by horses. Most lessons were soft spoken, and kind nudges that gave me multiple chances for do-overs. But nearly twenty years ago, on a hot summer day, I learned a doozy. That was the day I was tossed like a rag doll by Buddy, my husband's pretty Palomino.

Alright, I'm just going to say it. "Buddy" was a wildly inappropriate name for this horse. With his shifty eyes, and iffy demeanor, it was no surprise when he began testing our new trail wrangler beyond her ability.

I rushed in with a big attitude, and not the slightest curiosity to see why the horse was blowing up.

"How about I hop up so I can teach him a lesson?"

Old, seasoned horsemen are like sages. Their ageless advice has prevented countless mishaps – when heeded.

"Only fools share the saddle with anger or arrogance."

Clearly, I missed that one.

The moment I mounted up, Buddy lifted off, bucking, kicking, and twisting. Just like the bronc in the movie "Eight Seconds."

My only hope to regain control was to dive over the horn, grab the shank of the bit, pull it hard towards my stirrup, and force him into circles. But the trick was to sandwich my attempts between his vicious bucks.

When I lost my stirrup, it all went black.

I could hear the sage echoing, "When tossed, get up, shake it off, and mount back up. If you don't, the horse wins, and you've created a bigger problem than just your bruised ego."

Using both hands to push against the hard packed ground, I hoped to rock back on my battered bottom. But the crunching sound in my shoulder, piercing pain in my side, and burning sensation running up my back told me this wasn't just any fall. There was no shaking this one off.

When my staff got to me, I was able to lift my face off the ground only enough to mumble, "Call an ambulance, but tell them no lights or sirens. It'll scare the horses."

So many things were broken, torn, and bruised that day. Two of my ribs, my collar bone twice over, a ligament in my back, my pride, and confidence.

But what hurt the most was knowing my reckless choice caused an incalculable consequence – my new fear of horses.

Time was the enemy. If too much passed before resolving my fear, this accident may not only change me, but alter our dreams for Trinity. After all, how could I lead our vision if I was terrified of it?

Months of persistent and agonizing shoulder pain sent me to an orthopedic specialist. The scans showed the dual fracture wasn't healing, and even worse, it showed no signs of trying. The only remedy was a titanium plate.

The evening before my procedure, I stood on our deck, soaking up the panoramic view of Trinity with its miles of white fencing, and acres of green pastures with beautiful grazing horses. Then reality rushed in to remind me I needed two good arms to do the work God called us to do.

I pleaded for Him to heal me.

Waking in recovery, I slurred, "How did it go?"

My husband smiled, "You did great hon, but they didn't do the repair."

"What do you mean? They didn't fix my shoulder?"

"They didn't need to—your bones were healed. No one could believe it. It's really a God thing. The scan showed it wasn't healed two days ago, but it is now!"

Praise God!

As I grew older and gained a more distant perspective on that event and others, I realized my relationship with my horse is remarkably similar to my relationship with God. They were both created and maintained by a succession of choices and consequences.

The time, energy, and love I chose to pour into each created the consequence of connection, relationship, and trust.

Horses play a monumental role in the work we do at Trinity. Just as God gives us free will, we do the same for our herd. They tell us if they want to work by either walking away or submitting. It makes all the difference in the world.

Have you ever been tempted to test the biblical theory of free will? Is the reward worth the cost?

I invited one of our veterans to step into my boots to conduct his own free will test.

Staff Sergeant S. M. Tapper, a three-times deployed Army veteran, was a logistics specialist. He made sure things landed where they were needed, or people died. Ammunition, information, and rations. They all mattered. They were all his assets, and all his to allocate.

After twelve years of perfecting his system, Samuel's worldview evolved into a stream of complicated transactions. His "I, me, and mine" ethos prompted a violent confrontation with his wife's demands of "we, us, and ours."

He came to us as a parolee, seeking a new start after attempting to drown his demons in a fifth of Jack Daniels for the umpteenth time.

Drinking, driving, and one's demons usually cause life-changing consequences. For Samuel, it was a conviction of aggravated assault, and his sixth DWI that sent him to prison for double digits.

Equine Assisted Therapy is an experiential model. Our clients learn-by-doing. We blend relationship and skill building with challenging activities to encourage insight and change.

These horse-based activities reveal our client's unhealthy patterns, counterproductive behavior, and emotional discrepancies that cause conflict. And conflict inevitably causes consequences.

After a few weeks of getting to know his horse, we began Samuel's session with a scant directive.

"You have a halter, a schedule, and a choice. Will you rely on your halter or your relationship to get Gunner to the barn?"

Samuel took the task seriously, "If I'm on the tick-tock, then I'm using the tools that will keep me on the right side of it."

He quickly walked out to Gunner, slid the halter on, pulled up hard to free him from his hay, and continued the pressure until the horse began to walk with him.

Halfway to the barn, Gunner's pasture mates noticed he was gone, hollering out to him. The horse stopped, turned, and started back towards the herd, but Samuel refused his request, snapping hard on the lead to stay on schedule, and meet his goal.

When they reached the barn, Samuel barked, "mission accomplished," as if reporting to a superior officer.

Refusing to be distracted, we asked, "How was that for you? How did it feel?"

"Feel? I didn't feel anything, I just got the job done. You asked me to bring the horse to the barn. He didn't want to come, so I made him."

"Did you do anything to strengthen your connection with Gunner? To build on your relationship before you asked him to follow you?"

"No, why would I? I'm in charge, and he's my subordinate. It's not a negotiation. He does what I ask. Period."

My ministry partner and I exchanged a quick and quiet glance, knowing if this is how he managed his marriage, no wonder it seemed to be over.

We knew it was imperative to challenge his pattern of thinking, so as Samuel and the horse entered the arena, we pushed back.

"Let's have you partner with your horse to do an activity that demonstrates teamwork. You can do anything that shows us you can work as a unit."

Samuel seemed irritated as he stood staring at the horse. Shifting his weight from side-to-side, and kicking the sand, he finally asked us to repeat the instructions.

Before we had a chance to reply, Gunner gave a forceful snort, as if to say "I'm out!" and trotted off.

Sprinting to catch up to him, Samuel grabbed a handful of Gunner's mane. The veteran set his heels deep in the footing, as if that would be enough to stop this 1500-pound gelding. But instead, he learned a lesson in weight differential, force, and momentum. As his grip broke, he landed face down in the sand.

We smiled and asked, "Do you want to try something else?"

He stood up, brushed off the dirt and embarrassment, and insisted, "No, I think we worked great as a team! Don't you?"

We were speechless.

The following week Samuel blew in, creating a monster dust cloud as he skidded to a stop.

"Now that Gunner and I have this team-thing down pat, what're we going to work on today?"

"You're going to test the concept of free will."

"Free will? What's that?" Samuel shrugged.

"God gave us free will – the freedom to make our own choices. Good or bad. He could've made us like puppets, so we only did what He wanted, but He didn't."

Samuel chucked, "Seems God needs to reread the handbook on the Chain of Command."

Without response to his thought, we continued, "You'll have no halter. In fact, no tools of any kind. It's the only way to make this a real test."

Samuel looked confused, "But if I can't use a halter, how do I make him follow me?"

"That's the point. It's not about demanding he follow you – it's about stirring his desire to follow you. He has to want to. You're giving him free will."

As we slowly approached the herd, my partner and I stopped to give Samuel enough space to analyze his mission and prepare his approach.

The veteran began calling to Gunner like a dog. "Come here boy! Come on!"

He slapped his leg, tried different gestures, and finally resorted to bribing him with some left-over lunch lying on the ground.

No luck. The horse needed a compelling reason to choose Samuel.

After nearly twenty minutes of trial and error, we decided to put Samuel out of his misery with a few tips in the form of questions.

"What if you gave Gunner an irresistible reason to follow you? What if you did something for him that he can't do for himself? Can you make yourself indispensable to him? Do you think that might make a difference?"

Samuel finally caught on, and slowly approached Gunner while he was grazing. The veteran softly stroked the horse from the top of his neck, over his back, and followed his dorsal stripe to his tail.

"Do something for the horse that he can't do for himself," Samuel quietly repeated.

Taking several steps back, Samuel surveyed Gunner's entire body, searching for the spot where he was tormented the most.

He found it! Hidden between his two front legs, where his barrel meets his ribs. It's where the gnats dig in and gnaw all day.

Gunner's neck stretched to giraffe-length, his big lips quivered uncontrollably, and his eyes rolled back to all white as Samuel began to scratch. Eureka!

We knew it was the perfect time to start our test.

"Samuel, stop scratching, and start walking towards the barn."

He shot us a sharp look, and said, "Why? I just found his sweet spot, and he's loving it. What if he doesn't follow me? Then I fail the free will test, right?"

Samuel reluctantly complied, but was disappointed when Gunner immediately resumed munching, as if his scratching didn't matter.

It wasn't until Samuel got nearly forty feet from Gunner before the horse lifted his head, noticed the veteran was gone, and chose to leave his mates to follow him.

This was truly remarkable! Gunner left safety and food, two of the most important needs in every horse's life, so he could follow a human he knew for only a few weeks.

The horse trotted up to Samuel, but instead of speeding by, he slowed to match the veteran's pace. Shoulder to shoulder, they finished their walk to the barn. No halter needed. *Simpatico.*

"Samuel, how did it feel this time? Which experience would you rather have?"

His tear-filled eyes told us the experience stirred him to the core.

As he paused to regain his composure, I was praying he'd answer from his heart, instead of his head. I was praying he'd remember all he learned about the power of connection, relationship, and trust.

Would he "make good choices"?

Would he choose the session when he used the halter to control the outcome, or the one when his connection with Gunner determined the outcome?

Would he choose the one when he sacrificed his relationship with Gunner for the sake of the goal, or the session when he realized the goal was to sacrifice to build the relationship?

And would he still choose his "I, me, and mine" mentality, instead of trusting God and the heart of his horse to help him find peace, joy, and purpose?

"I choose the one when Gunner chose me! When he left his friends and trotted up to me. When we were walking so close it felt like we were one. I choose that one. I chose him, because he chose me!"

"I'll bet that's just how God feels when we choose Him," I said.

"Will you tell me more about the God you follow? The one you talk to like a friend. I want to know Him."

"Yes Samuel, we'd love to tell you more about Him."

People often ask why I think horses are such good healers? Why do they seem to know what we're thinking, feeling, and how they can help?

It's simple. Because they're good readers. They read our body language to learn what we're feeling, and they read our heart to learn why.

Our life's story is an accounting of our choices, and their consequences. When we choose to trust God over our need to control, we experience His glorious presence and guidance over our life. We experience the hope, peace, and purpose He meant for us.

And when we choose to bond with a horse, they help us become better humans.

Life presents choices when we least expect them. Will we lean in, or move away? Slow down, or speed by? Embrace, or resist? Confess, or deny?

Will we welcome the opportunity to bring someone closer to Christ? We have free will, you know. What will we choose?

Father, thank You for the gift of free will. Please help us to use it wisely, and "make good choices." And when we get tossed by life, please pick us up, shake us off, and send us back out in Your name. To do Your work. To glorify You. In Your precious name we pray. Amen.

Author Note

"Maybe our choices, our ability in every situation to choose, is one of God's greatest gifts to us. In a sense, not to choose, merely to let our lives drift along, is to be unfaithful to the great gift of life God has given us. When I choose, when I walk down one road and not another, particularly if it's a difficult and demanding road, it's my way of giving thanks to God for the gift of life and freedom.

"Jesus Christ is the Good Shepherd who beckons ordinary people to change directions in their lives, to come forward, to walk down the road with him. Thus a relationship with Jesus begins with a choice."
Rev. John D. Payne, St. Stephen's Episcopal Church 1/23/16

Chapter Sixteen
Ribbons of Redemption

"Mom, what happened to you? You've changed so much. You're not my mother anymore!"

What an explosion of contrast. From a Midwest mommy to a US Marine soldier.

Tanya went from putting satin ribbons in her daughter's braided hair on Monday to training "know-nothings" in the Middle East on Friday.

The whiplash was brutal.

Each send-off and return became harder. Each deployment further ripped the family fabric until there was little left to stitch together. Each mobilization made the memory of her suburban life less recognizable. Just a distant desert mirage.

Three tours of living in the largest sandbox in the world corrodes everything above ground. But that's nothing compared to what that environment does to a person's psyche and soul.

Kyla was four years old the first time Tanya answered the call. Nine years old on the second, and now twelve when her mother returned, this time for good.

The veteran blew into her mother-in-law's home, expecting things to be as she left them. But the unanswered letters and promised-but-never-returned phone calls changed all that.

"You promised you wouldn't just show up and jerk me out of everything I finally got used to. I have a life here with Grandma," Kyla said, crying. "You don't know what it's like. I'm not leaving! Not again!" "Grab your things and pack up. Make no mistake, young lady, we're both leaving," Tanya demanded.

When Kyla heard her mom was coming home, she prayed it would be the version of her mother who used to bake cookies, cheer from the bleachers at her volleyball games, and wipe her tears when the schoolyard bullies wore her down.

Tanya's role in the Marines was to train new enlistees on communication, procedures, and allocations. How to talk, what to do, and where to go. No wonder she was brassy and belligerent.

Communication is a big thing. My dad always said, "There are no problems except communication problems. Wars were started, divorces were filed, and students were left untaught because of bad communication."

At Trinity, communication between a horse and a human usually happens very organically. That's how we prefer it. But there are those times when a particular horse could bring a particular perspective to a particular struggling veteran.

Shamrock was the horse, "ground driving" was the eye-opening perspective, and Tanya was the veteran.

Our miniature horse partners are often just what the doctor ordered. They're playful, so learning and pushing through barriers feels rewarding. They're persistent, so the breakthroughs are unmistakable, and their size and stature are unassuming, so they can fly under the radar like a stealth bomber honing in on its target and delivering a winning drop.

Shamrock was always ready to serve up her masterclass in communication.

Ground driving is a technique where a person stands twenty or so feet behind a horse with long lines clipped to the horse's halter. Your *message* needs to travel from your hands all the way down the long loose ropes to your horse. It must accurately tell your horse what you want her to do. If you've never tried this, it's much like the old-fashioned telephone game. The message is clear as a bell when sent, but it's often something entirely different when it's received.

A flawed system, you say?

Oh, heavens no. It's perfectly *imperfect* for our needs.

But we made it harder for this Marine. Tanya had to communicate with her horse using such precision that she could guide Shamrock through an obstacle course with *en route* choices and varying terrain.

And to top it off, this veteran unknowingly would have been the designer of her own course.

Tanya followed us into the pasture with long sweeping steps, rubbing her hands together, and said, "Okay...let's see who looks like they can handle me."

Finding a horse that can *handle* the veteran is the farthest thing from our minds and the opposite of what we look for. A horse that pushes, challenges, and shows defiance serves our process well.

"Here you go, Tanya. Here's the horse you'll be working with," I said, offering no wiggle room.

"No, ma'am. That horse is way too small and could never take what I've got to dish out."

I said nothing, not wanting to let the cat out of the bag as to who would be *handled*.

We know that a person gets worn out and worn down after three deployments. Interests and relationships don't matter to them as they did before. Losing things isn't as heartbreaking as it used to be. Even if it was a husband, mother, and now maybe even Tanya's daughter.

"Everyone says I've changed so much. That I don't listen or even try communicating anymore. What do they expect? I am who I am. I am who three tours in the Marines made me into. If they don't like it—that's tough. I'm not changing. I can't change," the veteran said sternly.

Quickly pivoting, I said, "Let's start with a little grooming. Grab the brush and mane comb and go to work on the horse."

"Look at her hair!" she exclaimed. "It reminds me of my daughter. I used to brush and braid her long, beautiful hair every night. It was our time to be together. We both enjoyed it."

"When's the last time you did that? Spent time together—just to be together?"

"It's been forever. Not since I came home from my second deployment. Kandahar or Kabul—take your pick. They'll both sandblast your femininity and motherhood clean off your bones. Your soft and kind side becomes hard as the concrete-like sand we lived on."

My therapy partner and I noticed her unemotional tone.

"We female Marine leaders straddle two worlds. To be considered as competent as our male counterparts, we have to mirror them. Walk like them, talk trash like them, and bury our emotions like them." Tanya continued, "But then there are times when you have to muster up all the angry emotions you can and push back HARD—I mean with everything you got—just to keep them off you."

The veteran groomed the horse for less than a minute and abruptly stopped and threw the brush and comb in the grooming bucket.

"I'm done. That's a waste of time anyway."

"Is it?" my therapy partner asked. "Why do you say that?"

"I don't need to make friends with this horse for me to teach it what's what," she snapped.

"But what if the horse has something to teach you? Having some kind of relationship with her might come in handy, don't you think?"

The concept of a horse having the audacity to teach her anything was as foreign to her as the faraway places she's served in for so many years.

A few weeks passed before Tanya decided she might as well cooperate and "get this over with" so she could prove to her husband and daughter that she was trying to put the pieces back together.

"Your mission today is to design an obstacle course. One that you envision your enemy having to maneuver through, so no cake-walks allowed," I said straightforwardly. "You can use anything in this arena to build it."

She scoffed it off and went about gathering things from the arena periphery, mounding it in the center of the space. Pool noodles, mounting blocks, ground poles, cones, barrels, jumping standards, hula hoops, and even the tote of ropes and ties. It all got thrown in a heap.

The veteran stood motionless for two or three minutes, then started circling the pile, hand on her chin, looking like she was waiting for inspiration to hit her.

It took her the rest of the session to create it. But when it was done, this obstacle course was a tactical masterpiece of over, under, around, and through.

"So, tell us about the course you designed. Give us a tour and explain what the objects represent."

"I guess it looks like my life," she said, surprised. "The bright cones are the people who used to be important in my life. The ground poles are the path I took by going into the Marines. The hulas are the hotspots in my life that are always teetering on destruction."

She was clearly on a roll, so I waited until she was ready to stop.

"And the curvy ropes are choices I could've made, probably should have made, but didn't."

No wonder she was knee-deep in struggles. The landscape of her life was like the Marine Corps Tarzan Course. Not created to simply challenge the prospect but to fail them.

"Well done," I said.

"So, now what?"

"Now, you ground drive your horse through your course."

"What? You never said *I* had to go through this course. You said, my *enemy*."

"Sometimes they're one and the same," my partner added.

Cooperation is always a byproduct of the connection and relationship between a horse and a human. It'll become glaringly obvious how important the grooming process is. But because Tanya short-stopped that relationship-building phase, this mission might resemble herding cats more than ground driving a horse.

"Stand about fifteen feet behind your horse. Grab the ropes and steer your horse through your course," I said, purposefully minimizing the task.

The veteran started strong. Both hands gave ample and equal length to the horse as they walked on.

But then, the communication gap grew. The horse stopped, and the vet started slapping the ground with violent whips of the ropes. Instead of this telling the horse to keep going, it did the opposite. Shamrock knew exactly what she was being asked, but she refused to respond to such aggression.

The veteran repeated slapped several more times, some with more vigor than others, but all attempts produced the same—nothing.

The veteran drove herself right into the middle of a communication conundrum. But her training came in handy. Tanya regrouped and pulled some of the rope in, making a tighter, more controlled length.

The vet asked the horse again, only this time she used her voice, hands, and her forward energy—the perfect trio.

"Okay, Shamrock, let's go," she said, her tone raised.

When Tanya kissed to the horse, the journey of ten-thousand steps began.

The veteran made it to the cones and slowed only momentarily when they came to the hulas. Tanya raised her energy and pushed the horse forward to the ground poles. The team moved on to the "should-have, could-have" zone, and Shamrock stopped dead in her tracks. In fact, she started backing up, going far outside the course.

No matter what the veteran did, the horse didn't move from there.

Obviously, this was an area that needed attention. The horse put it in park, and the veteran put it in the past.

"I should've made different choices. I should've stayed to work it out with my husband instead of accepting the third assignment, but I didn't know how to. If I had, maybe he wouldn't have left, and we'd still be a family."

The veteran was fighting to hide her tears.

"I could've called Kyla when I promised. I could've sent her cards. But it was my way of controlling my emotions. I just couldn't handle hearing her voice or putting my real feelings down on paper. I couldn't afford to open my heart like that." She finally looked at us.

That was our opening.

We stepped in and began, "Tanya, what do you want to do now? You can't go back in time, but you can do things differently going forward."

"I need to *figure out* how to do things differently. To be a loving mom and wife again."

"That's why you're here," I said softly.

The following week started fresh. Tanya came with a smile and a bounce. She eagerly shared her conversation with her estranged husband and how hopeful they both were.

"Are you ready to try your course again?" I asked, matching her energy.

"Yup, but first, I need to spend some time with Shamrock, so she knows I care about her. So she knows we're a team."

God is so good. We didn't flip that switch—He did.

After the veteran groomed Shamrock, the horse looked show-ready.

"Okay, Shamrock, let's do this. I know we'll do better this time," Tanya said with evident confidence.

Off they went, rounding the curves and smashing the straightaways just like the Indy 500. But they went into a spin when they reached the "should-haves"—again.

We raced in from the sidelines like her pit crew and asked, "What barriers are you coming up against when you reach that spot? What's stopping you from moving past it?"

"I just keep thinking about all the things I gave up, did wrong, and wish I could do over. But I can't. I need to let them go, don't I?" She lowered her head.

"You do, but we'll help you," my partner said.

"Tanya, before you come back next week, write down all the things you regret. The things you wished you could do differently, and bring the list with you."

She agreed, and off she went.

When the veteran arrived the following week, she looked worn out. This is a grueling process at times.

But God delivered an amazing plan.

"Tanya, let's have you comb Shamrock's mane again, only this time, braid it like you used to do for Kyla."

She went at it with the passion of a doting mother. When done, she had twelve perfect braids.

"Next to you is a basket of satin ribbons and markers. Write one thing from your list of regrets on each ribbon, then tie it to a braid," my therapy partner instructed.

Tanya started cautiously but then found her groove.

"Can I do more than twelve? I have more on my list."

"Do as many as you want. There are plenty of ribbons."

Writing down regrets, failures, and things you wish you'd done differently is a cathartic process. There's a release that happens when you transfer those thoughts from running wild in your brain to wrangling them down on paper. They lose their power. They become words on a page, not monsters in your mind.

When she finished, the horse looked like she had stepped off the movie set of "Spirit" with a rainbow of ribbons waving in the wind.

"I did it, and it feels amazing! It's like the weight of the world came off my shoulders. I don't have to protect my heart by being cold and distant. I can love again! I feel like my life will be better—no—that it will be the way I've prayed it would be. Full of love, tenderness, and peace."

That's the deliverance God provides. That's nothing we can do. We're merely the conduit. Our Father is who orchestrated this *homecoming*.

"Tanya, there's one more thing you need to do. Untie your horse and walk with us."

We took her to Shamrock's pasture.

"We're so thankful God transformed your ribbons of regret into your *ribbons of redemption*. God took on your misdeeds and gave you a clean slate."

"Thank you, Jesus!" we all chimed in.

It was time to release Shamrock. The veteran slipped the halter off and gave the horse a pat.

Shamrock took off like a bullet, taking all the ribbons, all the burdens, and all Tanya's regrets with her. Never to be seen again.

Over time, we know the ribbons fall off and become part of the dust, dirt, and soil of the pasture. We think that's how it should be.

"From dust to dust."

Lord, You move in such remarkable ways. You enter our time and space and anoint it with Your presence and purpose. Thank You for taking our wrongs and righting them, so we can live close to You on earth as we will in Heaven. Amen.

Author Note

Thoughts on Communication:
- Lack of communication breeds assumptions about the other person's thoughts or feelings. Assumptions are more often than not incorrect.
- The biggest communication problem is we don't listen to understand. We listen to reply.
- Lack of communication leads to misunderstandings. Misunderstandings turn into disagreements. Disagreements turn into conflicts. Conflicts turn into arguments. Arguments turn into fights. Fights turn into wars. The cycle repeats until effective communication begins.
- Before we speak—we should THINK.

  T – Is it true?

  H – Is it helpful?

  I – Is it inspiring?

  N – Is it necessary?

  K – Is it kind?

Chapter Seventeen
The War Called Grief

Denial, anger, bargaining, depression, and acceptance. Grief is not courteous enough to follow this tidy string of words so when you reach the fifth, we're done. Hallelujah. Grief journey over.

That's a far cry from the truth.

My husband and I know the stages of grief intimately. Almost four decades ago, a rare one-in-three-million heart condition stole the life of our first child at 188 days. Our unresolved and incomplete grief tried to steal the 365 that followed.

Military veteran Captain Harold Tipper took his turn traveling through these five hellacious stages.

He even visited more than one — more than once.

But he, like we, and so many others found the fifth to be the thorniest.

Acceptance was the one that caused the most inconceivable contradictions, and waged an all-out war in the depths of our psyche. This is the war called grief.

This battle is between the necessity to accept the loss of a loved one, and the inhumane deluge of guilt the survivor is flooded with the very second they do.

It's a dichotomy for the ages. The most painful game of Catch-22, and the war that takes the most faith to conquer, and often leaves the most questions.

Harold is a Marine veteran who spent more than his fair share in the rice paddies of Vietnam. He lost countless friends and comrades to enemy fire. And suicide.

His wife was not only his devoted advocate, but his fail-proof historian. She knew the dates of this veteran's assignments, transfers, injuries, commendations, and even reprimands.

But the one date Harold needed no reminder for was the day his son died. That one lived deep in his psyche.

Private E. C. Tipper was one of three casualties in a gone-wrong mission to secure an enemy communications tower.

"Eddy's team came in hot and things went sideways. My son was killed trying to evacuate his injured unit members. They made it. He didn't," Harold said in a level tone.

The veteran—Eddy's father—was changed from that day on.

"I have pretty bad nightmares. Had them ever since my boy was killed."

My therapy partner asked, "Could you describe them to us?"

"The worst one is where I'm in my son's unit and I know what's gonna happen. I know they're gonna take heavy fire, but nobody else knows."

I sat listening in suspense, watching Harold's face lose color.

"I'm trying to catch up to Eddy and tell him to get out of there, but I can't reach him fast enough. I'm running in thick mud. I couldn't save him."

"Harold, we're so sorry for the loss of your son and for that awful, recurring nightmare," I said.

"My wife says the nightmares are because I've never accepted Eddy's death. Do you think that's true?"

"It certainly could be. I know people who still grieve their loved one even after ten or twenty years. Incomplete grief can change your life even more than the loss of a loved one itself," the therapist stated. "You have to grieve fully so you can heal fully. At your own pace and in your own way."

This is a hard fact I've heard often. I've learned so many things about mental health and mental illness from the therapists on our team.

With every passing year, an untreated trauma digs a deep rut in a person's psyche. Replayed memories and the sensation of the vivid turmoil plows it deeper and deeper. So much so, that it's almost impossible to think about anything else.

Harold's been struggling with this nightmare for almost fifteen years. That's a cavernous rut.

The veteran walked into the arena where two horses stood ready for our first session.

Standing tall on the rail were five brightly colored traffic-like cones, a roll of duct tape, and a bold black marker.

"When you're ready, Harold, describe what you see," I said.

We needed to know if the vet's perceptions were in alignment with reality.

Harold jumped in. "One horse is tall and black, and the other is way shorter and brown."

"Watch them for a few moments, then give each of them a name," the therapist instructed.

"Okay, I've got it," he said with a smile. "I'm gonna call the brown one Harold, because he looks just like me. We both have brown hair and that horse is short and stumpy like me."

It felt good to hear some humor from him.

"The other horse I'll call Eddy. My son was like this one — tall, dark, and handsome."

My therapy partner said, "Now spend some time with each horse and get to know them. If you like, there are grooming brushes on the rail."

We were surprised when Harold spent the entire fifty minutes grooming the horses. It wasn't clear if he enjoyed the process so much, or if he was apprehensive about the next step.

Much to our surprise, the following week, Harold brought us lunch.

"We have a little fishing pond on our property. Eddy and I fished it often. We'd catch a stringer full right from the bench on the shoreline." Harold grinned.

We couldn't wait. Tearing the cover open, we dove in.

"Eddy made the bench in shop class years ago and gave it to me for Father's Day. I love that darn thing."

"This is scrumptious, Harold, "I said with my mouth full. "And the little powdered sugar dusted macarons? To die for."

The moment I said *die*, I looked for a hole to crawl into.

But Harold seemed distracted by the horses.

"Harold, have you heard of the five stages of grief?" my therapy partner asked.

"Sure have."

"Good. We're going to start there. Go ahead and rip off a piece of duct tape big enough to write the name of one of five the stages and then stick to whatever color cone you want," the therapist instructed. "Five cones — five stages — five labels."

"To help you out, there's a list of the stages next to the cones." I added.

He went right at it. Denial was blue, anger was yellow, bargaining was green, depression was red, and acceptance was black.

As he worked on labeling them, both horses stood at his side watching his every move.

"Next we'd like you to place the cones anywhere in the arena you want."

This time the vet stood at the rail for what seemed like forever. We thought maybe he felt uncomfortable with us watching and waiting, so we gave him some space. We moved to the other side of the arena and turned away from Harold. We didn't even sneak a peek to see where he put the cones.

When we turned back, we saw the vet had placed the cones haphazardly. No rhyme or reason that we could decipher — at least not that we noticed.

But we did notice the black cone — acceptance — was mysteriously missing.

We pushed on.

"Great job. Now choose one of the horses and lead it to whichever cone you'd like."

While the therapist was still talking, the vet turned to grab a horse. "When you're at a cone, tell us what you labeled it and how you're doing on that stage."

Harold seemed eager to choose his namesake for the first trip. The brown horse followed the vet to the cone, step-for-step.

Harold (the horse) stood alert at the veteran's side while he explained.

"The blue cone is denial. I guess I'm way past this one. There's no denying it — Eddy's gone," he said sharply.

The vet walked *Harold* back to the rail to switch horses. He led *Eddy* to the red cone.

"The red cone is depression. I've had a lot of experience with this one," he said, rubbing his chin. "When Eddy died, I didn't know if I could pull myself out of the black hole I'd sunk into."

While Harold described his depression, *Eddy* stood next to him, gently leaning in, his head hanging low.

"The depression, the darkness, and hollowness were unbearable," he sighed. "It's better now, but I can still feel it on a really bad day."

The veteran took his time as he led *Eddy* to the next cone. This one was on the furthest side of the arena.

The horse started in a trot, but slowed so the two were walking in perfect formation.

"The yellow cone is anger," the veteran said. "Yes, I admit it. Anger consumed me for a long time. It ate me up and spit me out... every day."

Eddy paced around the cone while Harold released his anger. The horse pawed the ground when the veteran's voice grew louder.

He ramped up. "I'm still angry. I'm angry when I think about the fact that Eddy's unit wasn't even supposed to be near that location. They shouldn't have been called in for that mission."

Harold was red-faced, with clenched fists.

"He wasn't supposed to be there when all hell broke loose." The veteran lowered his voice and continued, "But I realized being angry didn't help and scared my wife. So I learned to control it."

The horse settled when the veteran settled.

Harold led *Eddy* back to the rail and took the lead rope of the other horse.

Harold and *Harold* walked to the green cone.

"The green cone is bargaining, and boy did I bargain. I begged God to bring him back. I promised Him I'd do anything if only He would." The veteran's hands were wild now. "I told God I'd never swear again, never drink again, never take His name in vain again. I offered Him anything and everything of value I could think of."

Harold stopped mid-sentence.

The father took a deep breath, and continued. "I even begged God to take my life instead of my son's."

Eddy stood unusually close to the veteran while he recited his list. So close, Harold had to push the horse away from him at one point.

It seemed the horse refused to leave the man standing alone while he confessed his bargaining chips, and ultimately his ransom note.

The veteran walked over to us, as if he had finished the entire task, and said, "Well, how do you think I did?"

My partner didn't skip a beat. "You did very well with these four. You seemed to understand the impact they've had on your grieving process, and it sounds like you've worked through them successfully."

"But where's the fifth cone?" I asked him. "The black one that represents acceptance?"

As we scoured the landscape to locate the missing cone, *Eddy* left the rail.

The horse walked the entire distance of the arena to the edge of one of the wing walls at the very back of our indoor arena. The wing walls are out of the way enough not to be a hazard, but apparently the perfect place to hide something.

"Hey Harold, did you notice where *Eddy* is? Did you see what he found?"

The veteran seemed embarrassed.

"Yeah, I see *Eddy*. He's standing where I stashed the black cone."

My partner and I could see the emotion on Harold's face.

"I'm sorry I did that. I just wasn't sure I was ready to talk about that one yet."

"We understand. Looks like Eddy thinks you're ready. Maybe even overdue," I suggested.

We all walked over to *Eddy*. My partner, me, *Harold* the horse, and Harold the veteran and father.

The vet began, "I'm sure my son knew I loved him, I mean *love* him. I told him all the time. But it feels like if I accept he's gone, somehow that diminishes my love for him."

We could see how hard this was for Harold.

"I'm his father!" he shouted. "I'm still his father, and I should never give up on him."

He turned to the horse and began anxiously stroking his neck. "If I accept he's gone, I'm afraid that's the beginning of when I stop missing him, or stop remembering what he looked like."

The father teared up. "If I accept he's gone, will that mean I won't feel him in my heart anymore, or that I should stop wearing his dog tags around my neck?"

We knew he was on the cusp of the hardest one.

"If I accept he's gone, then he's really gone. Then he's really dead. That's why I chose the black cone as the acceptance one. Black means dead!" The father sobbed as he covered his eyes, and fell to his knees.

Eddy walked over to Harold and lowered his big beautiful head until it rested on the very top of his *father's* head.

It was as if *Eddy* was trying to tell his dad that they'll never truly be apart and it was okay to accept his death.

Seems the horse sensed Harold needed more convincing.

Then the most extraordinary thing happened!

Eddy folded his legs and slowly lowered himself to the ground, right next to his *father*. Right next to Harold.

The horse joined the veteran on the ground in solidarity, in support, and in deep love, delivering, once and for all, permission for his dad to accept his death.

Harold laid down next to his *son*, rested his arm over the horse's neck, and began to thank him through his tears — over, and over, and over.

I've worked with hundreds of veterans for well over ten years. Having a front row seat to countless transformations and "God moments" is a huge blessing.

But I can tell you, I've never witnessed anything like this before.

This was truly a gift from Harold's heavenly Father.

We continued seeing the veteran weekly for a handful of months.

Harold fully accepted Eddy's death and believed, whole-heartedly, that nothing ever would tarnish or change his love for his son.

On his last week, the veteran brought a photo to show us. It was of a small, simple hand-painted marker that he made for Eddy. It sat on a clearing next to the father and son's favorite fishing spot — the bench by the pond.

Harold said, "This way Eddy will know we're fishing buddies forever."

Father, You know the pain of losing a child. You lost Your son. You know when our sorrow is so strong it threatens to swallow us whole. Yet You are the soother of our soul. The caretaker of our heart. You promise that when we grieve, You grieve with us. When we mourn a lost loved one, You mourn too. And You lovingly remind us that those we've lost were Your loved ones first. You lend them for a season, and You promise we'll all come home to You at the hour of Your choosing. Amen, amen.

Author Note

A few years ago, I spoke to a group on grief and the loss of a child. It was difficult even after nearly four decades had passed since the loss of mine.

Grief is very personal, a mostly private journey, and can be transformational.

For me, the process of grieving fully and honestly taught me things about myself, my faith, about trust and God. Lessons only the pain of loss can teach.

Lessons like:
- How we manage our grief is what determines how long it takes us to see the light again.
- Our faith conquers our fears as we face the darkness of grief. It makes surviving the unbearable, bearable.
- In times of turmoil, God reaches for us. All He asks is that we take hold of His hand.
- When prayers go unanswered, it's not that God doesn't care or hear them. He has a different plan, one that is far beyond our human-size understanding.
- Trusting God is far more than just saying so. Truly trusting feels like the most reckless, mountaintop freefall. But without this trust-fall, we'd never know the blessedness of being caught and safely resting in the loving arms of our Savior.

If it weren't for our daughter Alexi's life and death and the transformation my husband and I went through, I doubt we'd have founded Trinity in 2002.

That leap of faith was the passion product of being so blessed by so many during a very painful time in our life.

We believe God calls us to bless others with the blessings we've received. We honor Him and our daughter by combining our love of horses, our deep devotion to kids in at-risk environments, and veterans struggling with PTSD by birthing something that helps others heal.

Chapter Eighteen
Better Than Before

"**B**e courageous enough to clarify! Only cowards skirt the facts. In the Army, if we didn't clarify, people died!"

This was my Dad's favorite pearl of wisdom. He retired as a Major, after twenty years in the Army. He had many of these pearls and shared them frequently. It was his way of helping us navigate life, to keep us headed in the right direction.

But this particular pearl reminded me to clarify for our new veterans; who we are, what we do, who leads at Trinity Equestrian Center, and for many of them, that they're forgiven.

Working with struggling veterans, watching how they bond with horses, and witnessing the miracle of how God changes lives is magnificent. But sometimes it doesn't happen that way. Sometimes we run into a veteran like Liam.

As a kid, Liam was a great athlete. As he grew, he honed his skills, sharpened his physique, and climbed to the ranks of a US Navy SEAL, his childhood dream.

"I'm a SEAL. I'm trained to carry out high-level assassinations when necessary, and hit within an inch of my target. It wasn't personal, just my job. My mission." After five deployments, his two failed marriages and three estranged sons were his personal collateral damage. He was done with the Navy, but it wasn't done with him.

During his assessment, we learned the details of his service, past therapies, but were puzzled why he'd travel three hours for our help. Then to confuse us even more, he proudly admitted he wasn't a fan of horses, saying, "I don't like them, and they don't like me."

Liam's demeanor caught us totally off guard. Every answer to every question dripped with sarcasm. It felt like a hostile game of ping pong. We'd lob a question over, he'd slam an answer back, throwing us a grin occasionally to soothe the sting.

By now, we had treated well over eighty veterans with complex Post Traumatic Stress Disorder. But we had never encountered anyone like Liam who so thoroughly understood what PTSD does to the human brain.

Hot and cold, angry and playful, charming and challenging, Liam traversed the emotional landscape in his first ninety minutes with us. He was brilliant, belligerent, and yes, a bully. His wit, and dust-dry sense of humor turned on us when he began a very graphic description of his state of mind. I'll warn you, it's gruesome.

"It's like I have a monkey sitting on my shoulder. He pries off my skull cap to get at my brain. Then he dips his skinny, crooked finger in and starts stirring, messing with my thoughts and emotions. Round and round he stirs. It makes me sick, confused, and paranoid."

I asked, "How often did this happen?"

"Did?" he blasted. "It still does. Almost every night."

It felt creepy, dark, and evil. Trying not to look spooked, we rolled on. "Let's talk about the three common service injuries—physical, emotional, and spiritual."

I explained, "Physical injury could be when someone loses a limb. Emotional injury often happens from a traumatic event and can cause depression or anxiety. And then there's spiritual, or moral injury. Veterans describe it as the guilt and shame they carry after doing something that violates their moral code. Maybe something they believe separates them from God."

I paused.

The other therapist added, "How about you Liam? Have you experienced any of these?"

Liam smirked, then gracefully replied, "I found the closer you get to God, the clearer your commitments are. And when you turn from them, or like me, abandon them, the conviction is crushing." He lowered his gaze.

"I know what I did," he said, "and I know God won't forgive me. My job was to kill my target, and I was good at it. God doesn't forgive that. Even if he did, I don't deserve it."

I gently replied, "Liam, no one is unforgivable. God will gladly forgive you if you ask Him. We'd be happy to pray with you about it."

He lunged forward in his chair, grabbed tightly on the armrests, locked eyes with me, and replied in his growl, "You can believe and do what you want when I'm not here. But the first time you two start praying for me, I'm gone. I won't be back."

Liam quickly shifted gears and began to detail his suicide attempts. He recounted how he was found, his many psych ward visits, and how his short list of friends got even shorter because of it.

Seemingly uncomfortable having revealed so much so fast, he broke into an awkward game of deflection, shooting us one salty joke after another. Not receiving the expected reaction from us, he grabbed his keys and phone, then darted for the door. He shouted over his shoulder, "I guess I'll see you next week."

We sank back in our chairs, trying to figure out what just happened. It felt like an emotional hurricane made landfall and ripped through our space.

I drew in a big breath and spewed, "Every challenge hides an opportunity, if you're smart enough to look for it."

"Another one of your Dad's pearls?" my work partner asked.

"Yup." I shrugged.

Not all veterans like working with horses. Often their size or a frightening childhood memory sour it. But not for Liam. He didn't like that their hide was dusty, and that they made a mess when they drank. It bugged him how their ears twitched for "no good reason," and how they always seemed to be watching him.

We soon concluded it wasn't the therapy he was seeking, it was the intellectual banter. He appeared to thrive on a good debate and enjoyed teasing us about our "incessant clarifications," while taunting the staff about his perception of God, his faith, and loss of it.

Everything with Liam was a negotiation. It was obvious from the start that our sessions with him would be different from all others. After a few rounds of sparring, we concocted a hybrid. We agreed to some talk-time, and he agreed to some horse-time. Fair enough.

Nearly ten minutes rolled as we waited for Liam to choose which pasture to start in. Was it fear, indecision, apathy, or his brand of defiance? No matter, we were determined to let it play out, not saying a peep as we stared at five gates.

Boots was the first horse to notice Liam. She's a larger than normal Quarter Horse mix. All horses—like humans—have a story. We discovered Boots was scarred with abuse and neglect. Hers took place in a ten-foot square stall, outlined with one single strand of electric wire. Some may consider her size an asset, but in this small box, it was a terrorizing liability. If she stepped forward, she'd get a ZAP! Then in fear, she'd bolt back, and ZAP! This continued until she surrendered, standing like some life-less Breyer statue. To Boots, stalls were dangerous, and humans were untrustworthy.

Horses consider trust a prerequisite for a relationship. They regard forgiveness as strictly conditional, and grant it in rations, only after trust is earned. It's hard and patient work for horses and humans. We can request forgiveness all day long, and it's only given if the giver is willing. Not like God. You ask from your heart, and He forgives.

Week after week, Liam and Boots spent time together, though never bonding. Liam kept his emotions safely tucked away, something he was very practiced at. It made sense. It was his emotional immunity that allowed him to do "his job."

It was Liam's fifth week when we got our first glimpse of what haunted him. As we walked down the barn aisle, we crossed paths with a young chore helper. She said nothing, just as all barn staff are instructed. It's a privacy thing.

Liam seemed unnerved seeing her, so I quickly reminded him that we had several staff members, and we'd occasionally cross paths.

I assured him no one knew anything about our "visitors." He nodded and mumbled, "I remember, but she looks just like her."

We seized the opportunity and asked, "Is that something you want to explore, Liam? We could do a talk week if you'd like."

"No!" he forcefully pushed back.

We entered Boots' pasture, Liam toting a curry comb and halter. As soon as the horse spied the tools, she bolted to the far end of the field. The veteran was more than happy to admit he wasn't looking for some "emotional thing" with her, but confessed he's fiercely competitive. "How many people have tried to halter this horse?" he asked.

"Probably ten by now." That was the carrot we needed to get him engaged.

When the veteran approached her, Boots turned and ran. He went at it again, but from a different angle. Still no luck. Then he took two steps towards her and stopped. Then two more, and stopped. This went on for nearly thirty minutes. Liam looked surprisingly patient and compassionate. We wondered if this was in his training, a warped take on bait and switch, or a change from within.

After his relentless attempts, ten feet still separated them. Liam saw it as defeat, I saw it as progress. Both Liam and Boots wrestled with PTSD, and I knew it wouldn't be an easy connection.

For the next several sessions, Liam opted for horse time, determined to halter and brush Boots no matter what. It became his mission, maybe even his obsession. But still nothing personal. It became a good old-fashioned stand-off.

Walking down the barn aisle, chatting with Liam about his week, we were delighted to detect his unusual upbeat mood. The therapist and I reached the back door with an extra bounce in our steps, but froze in disbelief when we swung it open. We saw Boots up at the gate, ears straight forward, and her entire frame facing us, offering a shy but intentional whinny.

"Is she actually waiting for me?" Liam asked skeptically.

"Maybe. Why don't you see if today's your day?"

He took a way too business-like approach. Far too confident and arrogant for her taste. As he got close enough to lay the lead rope over her neck, she turned and walked away. She didn't run, or even trot, she just strolled off. Knowing horses, I'd venture to say her change of heart was more about chastising him for his approach than her actual distrust of him.

On Liam's next visit, he saw the same young staff member in the parking lot. He shouted a few choice words and stormed into our office. He landed hard in the chair and barked, "I don't want to see her again! She looks just like her."

Taking a stand, my partner insisted, "Who Liam? Looks like who?"

"The young girl I killed." With his hands covering his eyes, he said, "She wasn't supposed to be there. I took aim at my target, and as I squeezed the trigger, the enemy pulled her in front of him. It was too late. I had no way of stopping it. I killed her."

We waited for him to unfold more of his story.

"I have nightmares every night. I see her face, all bloodied and torn. I can't make it stop."

For the first time we saw Liam's heart, his guilt, and even his remorse.

The therapist softly said, "To talk about it and admit its impact is the beginning of the healing."

Liam begrudgingly replied, "Yeah, I guess so, but it doesn't change anything."

The Holy Spirit poked me so hard, I almost fell off my chair. I blurted, "Seems like a good time for prayer, doesn't it?"

Liam rolled his eyes, cracked a sliver of a smile, and said, "Not yet." I took that as a huge sign of progress.

When he came the following week, he walked in with his chest fluffed out like a turkey and boldly reported, "This is the week." He seemed uncharacteristically confident that his goal of haltering, brushing, and walking Boots past the stalls and into the arena would happen today. Still no emotion or connection to the horse, just a job to be done.

The session went far beyond the normal fifty-minutes, but we didn't have the heart to call it quits. It took four attempts to halter

Boots, but to our surprise, brushing the horse looked natural for Liam, and soothing for her. Even walking to the gate seemed stress-free, until they reached the barn door. The horse's head shot up, her eyes tripled in size, and every bit of her 1500-pound body leaned back, refusing to enter. I took a step closer, signally to the veteran—clarifying—I was ready to grab the rope, but he waved me off. Liam lowered his head, slowed his breathing, calmed his voice, and said, "Let's go, girl." They both slowly walked in.

We were astounded as he led the horse from her right side. It's unorthodox for a horseman, but clearly showed his compassion as he tried to shield Boots from the stalls.

After entering the arena, they walked two laps in perfect tandem. Liam returned to the gate and announced, "There, it's done. She's good. I'm done with her. It was never personal, just my job, and I completed it."

Silently mortified, my partner and I hoped the experience with Boots would unlock more of Liam's heart. We prayed it would free more locked-up emotions and break down the stubborn walls he built so well. But it just didn't happen that way for him.

Liam continued to visit on-and-off for months. He'd take a sabbatical now and then, but made his way back when life became too bland, or he needed help sorting through things.

His trust in us eventually grew into sharing about his "ditched" relationships, odd jobs, family, and even his deepest desires, but he still refused to let us pray with him. We trusted being his silent prayer warriors planted seeds that eventually grew his desire to reconnect with God. We knew that was God's job, not ours.

The last time we saw Liam, he reported fewer nightmares, and even fewer visits from the creepy monkey. "It's not like it was before the Navy," he said softly. "But it's better than before, and I'm thankful for that."

As a treatment team, we pray for those titanic moments that change a veteran's life. Where they do a full about-face and turn from the turmoil they've lived, to the transformation God provides. That frequently happens at Trinity, but not always.

Sometimes, it needs to be enough to help a veteran accept that their past only defines them if they allow it. Or to help them believe they're the author of their own story, and with every breath they take, it's still being written. Or sometimes, it's enough when they're willing to consider that the things aggravating them the most just might be "pearls of wisdom" shared to help them navigate life. To keep them headed in the right direction.

And sometimes, just being "better than before" is enough.

Lord, you're our North Star, the navigator of our life's journey. We're all sinners and don't deserve your forgiveness, yet You offer it freely and unconditionally. Help all those who struggle in the darkness, step towards You in faith and be blessed by Your amazing grace.

In Jesus' name we pray.

Questions & Answers on Emotional Progress:
Q – If I want to measure my personal growth, how do I go about it?
A – It can be hard to gauge where we are, but the first step is to understand and practice self-awareness.

Q – What is self-awareness, and how do we get it?
A – It's a way to keep us grounded in reality and in the present moment. It doesn't let us water down or exaggerate the truth about ourselves, and our abilities. Having self-awareness means we see ourselves how we really are.

Q – How can I tell if I'm making progress? I feel like I'm better now than last year.
A – That's great! But another way of looking at it is to consider how things are going currently, and in the near past. You might be better than a year ago, or even a few months ago, but it's best to notice how this month is going, or this week, compared to last month or week. How does today compare to yesterday? Don't worry if you aren't sure you're making progress every day. It's normal to have ups and downs,

but best if you catch a negative pattern as soon as possible to avoid going downhill.

Q – I've heard if I can set a goal and reach it, I'm getting better. Is that true?
A – Yes, but it's important they're the right goals. SMART goals are the key. S-specific, M-measurable, A-attainable, R-relevant, and T-timely. Having specific goals lead you to answer what you are going to do, and how you will reach them. Make sure your goals state in detail what you're going to achieve. Make sure your goal is something you can actually attain. Set a goal that is relevant to you. Something you really want to achieve. Really define your WHY? That's what will make it happen. Give yourself a deadline for reaching your goal. A goal without a deadline is just a wish.

Q – How can I track my progress? Feels like if I could see it, I'd feel more motivate.
A – You're right. There are many ways to track your progress. Pick the one that fits you best, or a combination of them. A few suggestions: journaling, phone apps, your planner, or even a simple notebook. Track things like your success and failures, how you spend your time, your moods, emotions and feelings, thoughts, your habits (good or bad), your goals, and if you've achieved them.

Chapter Nineteen
You'd Do the Same

"I have your back—your 'six.'"
    Few bonds are stronger than that between comrades in the United States Armed Forces. It's the thread that connects each military branch to their high-held ethos and one another.
    Your *battle buddy* becomes your closest friend and your biggest responsibly. The pledge once exchanged as a requirement becomes voluntarily offered as honor.
    "I'd take a bullet for you, because you'd do the same for me."
    "If you get hit, I'll drag you to safety, because you'd do the same for me."
    "If I'm called to trade my life for yours, I'll do it, because you'd do the same for me."
    That bond will not be broken—and sometimes it risks breaking a marriage.
    Captain Paul Patton's ten-year Army pledge threatened his twenty-year marriage vows.
    "I don't trust you anymore, Paul. We used to be such a good team. You used to enjoy spending time with me—just me," his wife said sadly. "But now, your battalion buddies get all your attention. If one calls—you're gone. It doesn't matter what time, where we are, or what we're doing. You're there for them," she said adamantly.

His reply? "You don't understand, hon! Those buddies you complain about are the reason I'm still alive. And I'm the reason they're alive. We promised we'd always have each other's back. Always. I can't just ignore his call. He needs me. I have to go," Paul said apologetically.

Paul left his wife in disbelief and headed for his buddy. He pounded on the door of his battle buddy's apartment. It was locked, but that wouldn't stop him.

The veteran lowered his shoulder and drove it into the solid wood door. He nearly fractured his shoulder, but blasted it open on his third attempt.

There he was. Sprawled out on the couch, bottle in one hand, cell phone in the other.

"Brenden! Bren, dude, come on. Wake up!" Paul hollered while shaking him.

"Paul...Paul, you came! You really came," Brenden said, slurring his words.

"Of course, I did. What did ya' think? I'd just leave you hanging? We promised. Remember? Man, you need help! You can't keep doing this. One of these times you're gonna go too far and it'll be over."

"I don't wanna die. I just don't know how to live," Brenden said, tears falling down his cheeks. "It was easier to live through a day in the desert than it is here."

Paul couldn't argue.

"Did you get the call too?" Brenden asked. "Another one of our *unis* killed himself. That's three now! I just couldn't handle it."

"Yeah, I got it," Paul admitted. "It took me to my knees, but I didn't let it take me out. Maybe a few years ago—but not anymore. I learned how to handle my pain and grief. It's what's kept me alive. It changed my life."

No response.

Paul leaned closer to his friend. "I'm gonna call the place that helped me."

Brenden was too drunk to protest.

As they pulled into Trinity, Brenden started firing off questions.

"Paul, why are we coming here? What the heck, man. Why a horse place? You said you're taking me to the clinic that helped you, right?"

"I never said clinic—and this is the place."

My therapy partner and I met them in the parking lot.

"It's so good to see you, Paul. How ya doing?" I asked.

"Good—really good."

"Who's your friend?" I reached to shake his hand.

"This is Retired Lt. Col. Brenden Holmes. My Commanding Officer and longtime friend."

"It's good to meet you, sir," I said, a bit surprised at his rank. "And this is my business partner and senior therapist."

"He's the friend I called you about," Paul said. "Thanks for seeing us on such short notice."

"You know us, Paul. A vet referred by a vet takes the highest priority. Can I speak freely?"

"Yeah, no secrets here."

"Well then, what can we do for you, sir?" I asked the officer.

"The first thing is stop calling me sir. Those days are long over," he said firmly.

I asked, "Are they? You sure? How'd you like a tour of the place, sir… I mean Brenden?"

"Yes, ma'am," he said.

"Nobody calls me *ma'am* and gets away with it." I smiled broadly. "Toni works just fine. How much do you know about what we do here?"

"Only the little Paul told me. He said it saved his life."

"Paul did well in our program. He worked hard, made the changes he needed to, and walked out a new man. You could too, if you're willing to do the same."

"What I want is to stop seeing things at night that aren't there. Stop hearing voices from people who aren't there. My past won't stay in the past and it's raising havoc with my present." In a tight tone, he said, "Can you fix that?"

"It's not a matter of fixing it as much as it is understanding it, and in an odd sort of way, making friends with it. Calling a truce, so to speak."

I turned toward Paul to pull him into the conversation. "Our horses help with that, right Paul?"

"You won't believe what these horses can do, Brenden. I'm gonna wait in the lounge so you can properly begin," Paul said as he patted Brenden on the back.

We walked to our funnel—the confluence of seven pastures. The horses observe us, while we observe them.

Several curious horses came to their gates but none interested Brenden. Then he spied the gelding standing midway back in gate six.

"What about that one?" he said, pointing to Scout, a smaller than average maladjusted gelding. "He seems shy, but he's beautiful. Look at the color of his mane," the vet said.

"His name is Scout. We got him from a gal who rescues horses. Story is he came from the kill pen," I said cautiously.

"I know what a kill pen implies in the military, but what's your meaning?" the veteran asked straight up.

"Most livestock auctions have a designated area where animals are held if they fail to get a bid. They're marked *NV*—no value. After the auction they're trucked out to be put down."

"Scout survived the kill pen and ended up here, huh?"

"Yup. I think that's why he doesn't trust people. He holds a grudge. Can't blame him."

Over twenty years at Trinity, we've rescued more horses than we ever planned to. They usually have a traumatic history, but it's the history that makes them first choice when it comes to helping other trauma survivors.

"Sounds familiar. As a C.O., I picked out the underdogs and gave them extra support. That's how I met Paul. Any chance I could meet that horse?" the vet asked.

"He's all yours." I didn't share everything about Scout. For all I knew, Scout might warm up to him.

I wouldn't bet on it—but it was possible.

Brenden walked in and slowly headed for the horse. Scout looked like a statue until the vet got about ten feet from him. The gelding stopped chewing, pinned his ears, turned, and trotted away.

I noticed the compassion Brenden felt turn to disappointment when the horse repeated his refusals to engage.

"When the horse runs from me, does it mean he doesn't like me?" Brenden asked.

The answer has long become familiar by now. "It's not a matter of liking you. It's all about trust, or in his case, the lack of it." I hoped my words soothed the sting.

Weeks passed and still no connection grew between Brenden and Scout.

I asked Brenden the same question every week, knowing his disappointment dug deeper with every failed attempt. "Sure you don't wanna try a different horse?"

"No. This horse reminds me of one of my guys I once had. Tough background, piles of chips on his shoulder, and I'll bet if you looked hard enough he'd have NV marked on him too. So no, I'm not changing horses. He'll come around. I know it."

Nine weeks in, and to our surprise, the veteran came with a book in one hand and a coffee in the other.

"Looks like all you're missing is a nice comfy chair and you're set," I said, chuckling.

"No need for the chair, I saw one at the end of the barn that'll work just fine, if it's okay."

My therapy partner piped up, "You bet. We'll be at the gate if you need us."

"Hey, Brenden," I hollered, "what book did you bring?"

"*Mr. Roger's Quotes That Will Make Today a Beautiful Day*. He's got really good stuff in here. I thought Scout would enjoy hearing it."

We stood while the vet assembled his *lounge*. He found a stump just the size for his table and placed his bright white plastic chair within arm's reach. His coffee happily kept his book company while the veteran approached the horse.

"Good morning, Scout. Every morning I used to have my coffee and read one of my favorite books. It was the best part of my day. But lately my days have been pretty rough. So I hoped by sharing it with you, it might make us both feel better," Brenden explained. "I'll be over there." Brenden pointed to his lounge. "So if you wanna hear better... or anything, you can come closer."

My partner and I heard the entire monologue. To simply say we've never had a client do something like this before would be a gigantic understatement.

The veteran began reading, "'We speak with more than our mouths. We listen with more than our ears.'"

"'Who we are in the present includes who we are in the past.'"

"'Often, problems are knots with many strands, and looking at those strands can make a problem seem different.'"

By the time Brenden got to his last quote, the horse started inching his way towards him.

"'The world needs a sense of worth, and it will achieve it only by its people *(and horses)* feeling that they are worthwhile,'" he said, adding his own interpretation.

Brenden motioned for us to join him. We gladly obliged.

The vet put the book down, then he put his head down. He said, "Every one of my troops who were killed over there had value. And every one of my veterans who killed themselves back here had value. They just didn't see it. They didn't feel it—or believe it."

When the veteran raised his head, he found Scout standing next to him in the *lounge*.

Brenden slowly stood and turned to face Scout. The horse looked a bit spooked, with his wide-eyes and full whites showing.

But Scout didn't retreat. He just stood there— taking it all in.

"You, my friend, have value too," he said to Scout as his energy crept higher. "For someone to mark you *No Value* and put you in that pen was so wrong. They underestimated you."

Brenden closed the gap separating him from the horse. Scout stood still, even allowing the veteran to stand right next to him.

I shifted my weight, inadvertently signaling the horse that I was stepping closer. He pinned his ears but this time it was because of me. I noticed immediately, backed away, and the horse settled, becoming more comfortable in Brenden's presence.

It was the perfect note to end the session on.

Brenden was so encouraged by the progress he'd experienced he just had to share it with his estranged wife.

She'd left him when his alcohol became more important to him than she was. They said it was just a *break*, but she never held much hope that he'd get help and pull himself together enough to reunite.

Brenden dialed her and erupted, "Hi hon, I'm so excited! I was able to stand next to Scout today! I know it doesn't sound like a big deal—but it's a huge deal. He doesn't trust humans. But he's starting to trust me! Scout feels like everyone thinks he has no value. That he's worthless. It's taken me so long to get here."

"Is this where Paul got help?" she asked, her voice monotone.

"Yes! I've been going for weeks—actually months," Brenden said proudly.

"Is it helping you, Brenden? I mean really helping you?"

"Yeah, hon, it is. I know when I heard about the third suicide it sent me into a tailspin. I know it wasn't a pretty sight and I'm so sorry. But I haven't had a drink since I started coming here," Brenden proclaimed. "I feel better than I have in a long time."

She hesitated. Brenden continued. "Working with this team and Scout has taught me healthy ways to manage my grief, anger, and depression. Not just stuffing the feelings down and trying to drown them in a bottle. But talking about them—even praying about them," he said tentatively.

"They prayed with you?" his wife asked, sounding surprised.

"Yeah. I asked them to teach me how to pray like they do. Like God was my friend. And they did!"

"Well," she said. Then waited.

"They invited you to come with me next week. Would you? Would you come and meet my horse and see how good I'm doing? I'm gonna beat this thing, hon. I really am."

Brenden's wife came the following week and every one that followed. She continued until the veteran met all his treatment goals and graduated from our program.

Brenden and Scout became good friends. At the end of every session, the vet showered the horse with gratitude while brushing him from nose to tail. The vet always ends with a quote from the Mr. Roger's collection.

The vet told us, "At least I feel like I've helped save one that felt his life was worthless.

I couldn't save those lost in combat and I couldn't save the ones who committed suicide. But I feel like I saved this one—this horse—from living a life feeling he was of No Value just because he hadn't found his purpose yet."

What more could we have wanted?

"And in return, Scout saved me from being drowned in my grief and guilt, believing the lie that somehow I was to blame for losing my guys. That I was of No Value to my comrades, that I failed to 'have their six.' I know that's not true. Never was. I'm so grateful for that. Now I can move forward."

Over their time of working together, Brenden had shared dozens of Mr. Rogers quotes with Scout. The horse seemed to enjoy them as much as the veteran.

The one Brenden shared as a farewell was, "As human beings, our job in life is to help people *(and horses, of course)* realize how rare and valuable each one of us really is, that each of us has something that no one else has—or ever will have."

Father God, Your scriptures are overflowing with passages declaring how You hold us in high esteem. You say because we're created in Your image and by Your loving hand we have immense value. Thank You for forever reminding us of this. In Your name we pray. Amen.

Author Note

Fred McFeely Rogers was a uniquely insightful man. He was also a man who struggled with depression and a history of childhood trauma.

His quotes give us a peek into his heart. These are only a few samples of his wisdom.

➢ "The world needs a sense of worth, and it will achieve it only by its people feeling that they are worthwhile."

- "There is no normal life that is free of pain. It's the very wrestling with our problems that can be the impetus for our growth."
- "We all have different gifts, so we all have different ways of saying to the world who we are."
- "When we can talk about our feelings, they become less overwhelming, less upsetting, and less scary."

Chapter Twenty
Freedom Between Friends

As a country, we ask a lot from our veterans. We ask them to be willing to die for our way of life, our freedom, and our country.

If they manage to survive that, we ask them to return to their lives as if nothing has changed.

But it has. For them, *everything* has changed.

Because of their military experience and trauma associated with it, one-in-four veterans are homeless.

They are two times more likely to divorce.

Three times more likely to be unemployed and abuse alcohol.

Combat veterans are four times more likely to abuse drugs— and take their own life.

We have no idea what they've endured. We complain and overdramatize our occasional inconveniences as if they're grave events, while our service men and women face actual grave events—every day.

"It's aggravating when people complain about a few stupid potholes, when we drive over shredded bridges, not knowing if we'll fall to our deaths."

"I can barely tolerate it when people whine about how it's a hassle getting ready for work when we had no privacy. We had to share a bottle of water and sometimes even a toothbrush."

"I can't stand it when a co-worker gripes about having a bad night's sleep. We would have been thrilled to get three or four hours of sleep on the hood of our hummer."

"It drives me crazy when a friend can't understand why I drive fast under overpasses and refuse to slow down for a suspicious car."

"No one understands why we don't get excited for a friend who just got a new hot tub when we were lucky if we got a chance at a shower every few weeks."

"It's hard to stay quiet when people pray to God for a shiny new car when we were praying to get through the day without walking into another ambush, or losing another friend."

"I can't be compassionate when someone complains how hard it is to have a new baby in the house when I'm looking at a picture of our new premature baby girl fighting for her life on a ventilator... and I haven't even held her yet."

We ask so much of them. They sacrifice so much for us.

When they come back, they can't help but bring their insomnia, rage, flashbacks, depression, anxiety, isolationism, and suicidal tendencies with them.

Marine Corps Staff Sgt. Walter Perell was one of those who returned with a full load of struggles. He broke the silence with a hammer when he said, "There's no use in living."

The veteran's hands shook as he sat straight-backed, stirring his black coffee.

"When I was in the Corps, I knew what my mission was. What my purpose was."

The Marine paused, cleared his throat, and continued. "The first was to survive. The second was to complete the mission. So... I survived. Then I was discharged and came home to nothing."

My therapy partner and I sat silent.

"There're so many times I wished I had never made it back," the veteran said. "No one understands what it was like over there. I have nothing in common with my former life."

He pushed his coffee away so hard, it tipped and flooded the table.

"I have no clue what my purpose is. No clue how to feel alive again."

The therapist said, "Let's take a walk and introduce you to some horses."

Walter looked six-foot-something, and must have weighed nearly two-fifty, two-sixty, with zero fluff—zero. He was a commanding presence.

"Was there anything you enjoyed doing before you joined the Marines, Walter?" the therapist asked.

Sometimes circling back on passions once enjoyed can bring a vet back to life. It was worth a try to dig into Walter's past to resurrect something.

"Photography and drawing, but that was a lifetime ago," he said. "I never got good."

Hmm, interesting combination of tough and tender.

"Pasture four is a good place to start," I said, knowing we'd pass *him*.

If you Googled *War Horse*, you'd likely see an image like Zeus. He stood 19-hands high and was black as coal. His shoulders were as wide as a Hummer, his eyes could laser-cut concrete, and his legs were thick enough to serve as pillars to hold a building—or at least it seemed so.

His owner was a friend of ours who became ill and couldn't care for the horse anymore. My friend always said Zeus had a heart of gold—a perfect therapy horse.

We would see.

"Wow, look at him. He's huge. He'd make a great Marine," Walter said.

Zeus approached the gate and leaned against it to get a closer look at the veteran.

Clearly, this Marine was drawn to this horse. And that meant I'd be drawn into handling him. The horse had been with us only a few weeks, and no one had time to test him out yet.

Let me say, I'm no slouch with horses. I've been around the giant four-leggers for decades. But this horse even made me stand at attention.

"Have you ever been around horses, Walter?" the therapist asked.

"When I was a teenager. My friend had one, but nothing like this one. Nothing so majestic and powerful looking."

Veterans have a difficult time tapping into their positive emotions once they've had mixed military experiences. They've mastered the art of stuffing and covering the soft ones.

Negative emotions are far easier to access. Anger, fear, guilt, frustration, aggression, and hostility. But positive emotions are usually buried deep and need an excavator to unearth them.

That's why we were so encouraged when Walter's comments moved from desperation to observation. It showed he could access at least some of the desired emotions if he had the right motivation.

"Tell us more of what you see, Walter," my therapy partner said. "What draws you to this horse?"

"Can I go in with him to see him closer?" Walter asked.

"Of course," I remarked, quickly saying a pray for protection under my breath.

"Look at his eyes," Walter said, as he carefully brushed the horse's long forelock hair to the side.

Without warning, Zeus shifted his 2,000-pound frame. It sent the three of us into orbit.

Walter, the big, tough Marine. The mostly stoic therapist. And me— the *horse expert*. All undone by a simple movement by this horse.

As the veteran moved around the horse, I noticed Zeus softened his massive frame.

He lowered his head, rested a foot, licked his lips, and let out several deep breaths. All signs that Zeus not only tolerated our presence, but enjoyed it.

Walter's hands slid from the horse's withers down across his oversized barrel. The vet was mesmerized by how he could feel the energy move through the animal's muscles.

"Do you see how his muscles ripple?" Walter asked softly. "They're big and smooth at the start, but then taper and tuck under the next one. It's like a perfectly cast sculpture."

I think Walter spent far more time behind a camera lens and with a drawing pencil in hand than he led on. His artistic *eye* and expressive choice of words didn't just come out of nowhere.

"You have an amazing ability to see what most overlook," I said. "How about next session you bring your camera and catch some up-close shots?"

"Oh, I don't have any of that equipment anymore. When I went to the service, my mom threw my stuff out."

I wondered what message that sent to an aspiring artist about his talent and worth. Especially from his mother.

"No problem, I have a camera you can borrow."

"I know our session is over, but could I stay awhile to get to know Zeus better? I won't go into the pasture without you," the veteran said.

"Be my guest," I replied. "Just in case inspiration strikes, I'm gonna bring you a tablet and pencil."

On my way back, I saw Walter with his arms crossed and resting on the top rail of the gate, his forehead leaning against the giant gelding's.

When I walked back to meet my therapy partner, she said, "I'm encouraged to watch what happens when Walter connects with Zeus. The vet easily accesses his right-side brain. The side that governs spontaneity and creative thinking, instead of being stuck in his left-side, that controls his Combat-Marine thinking. That's neuro-plasticity in the making."

I love the mini-science and biology lessons from her.

"That's how his brain will learn to grow and be rewired. Spending time with Zeus will do this man a world of good," she finished.

The following week, we saw Walter's car in the parking lot, but didn't see him. We headed to the back pastures thinking maybe we'd find him by *his* horse.

Sure enough. There he was. He positioned the chair I left for him in just the right light to do some sketching.

"You beat us out here, Walter," I said with a big smile, handing him my camera. "Oh good, you found your drawing tools."

"No, I bought new ones. Zeus deserved a fresh start. So do I," the veteran said without looking up from his pad.

We knew God was on the move.

"Today's the day you get to halter this big guy and walk him to the indoor arena. How about it?"

"No thanks. Not inside," Walter said firmly.

The therapist asked, "Are you concerned about the safety of walking him in? If you are, don't worry. Toni will make sure everything goes well."

"No, no, I'm not afraid of him at all. He's calm and kind."

I was impressed by his confidence, but curious about his refusal.

"The light out here is perfect for taking photos and sketching him," Walter said. "But I sure would like to take Zeus for a walk in this gorgeous sunshine, if that's okay."

The veteran took the halter and held it as high as he could reach. Walter had no hope of reaching Zeus's tower-like range without the horse's cooperation, or a ladder.

With lowered head, the horse allowed the vet to slide his halter on, and off they went. Zeus with his huge, lumbering stride, and Walter, savoring every moment.

We made our way around the perimeter of the south property. Twice. There was no tiring them. The two fast-friends walked, talked, stopped for pictures, then walked and talked some more.

"Walter, if it's okay, I'd like to take a few photos of you and Zeus," I said. "There're some great shots I could catch that you might enjoy."

Photography is one of my passions. Catching the perfect *suitable-for-framing* photo is worth the challenge. Over the several weeks, I caught them all.

Out of left field, Walter asked, "What do you think God's gonna say to me when I meet Him?"

"What do you hope He'll say?" I asked.

"That He forgives me. Forgives me for the things I've done. I wasn't a boy scout. The military made sure of that."

My therapy partner asked, "Have you asked God for His forgiveness, Walter? God forgives anyone who sincerely asks."

"No, I haven't. I don't think He'd forgive me if He knew all that I've done."

Zeus and Walter stood shoulder-to-shoulder, as if they were ready for roll call.

"I mean, I'm not a monster or anything, but what I did, no one would forgive. Not even God."

"Walter, He already knows everything you've done—what was required of you and what wasn't. He knew it before you even did it. He knows how you feel about it, and how heavy it weighs on your heart."

Zeus stood facing Walter. The horse lowered his massive forehead and placed it on the veteran's chest, covering the entire space.

The image was stunning. It was as if Zeus knew Walter's heart needed to be released from the grief, guilt, and shame.

It's been said that war can either showcase our humanity or showcase our *lack* of morality.

Missions and orders—even difficult orders—are obeyed. People are injured and killed. Both sides suffer and are forever changed. It takes an act of God's grace to forgive, redeem, and transform.

"Do you want us to pray with you, and ask God's forgiveness?" I asked.

"Would you?"

"Father, your son, Walter, is asking for your forgiveness. His heart is being crushed by the weight of his guilt and shame and—"

Walter broke in, "God, I'm not sure what to say to You, but I want You to know I'm really sorry for what I did, and what I didn't do. There are things I should have stopped, but I didn't. Please forgive me and help me be a better man. Amen."

Zeus didn't move a muscle during Walter's prayer. The horse held space for the heart-healing to take place, and it did.

"What's next? What do I have to do to make sure this works?" the veteran asked.

"What worked? God's forgiveness?"

"It can't be that simple, can it?" Walter asked.

"Yes. God knows your heart. There's no more to be done."

"I feel like I can't lose today! So, can I try something with Zeus?" Walter asked hesitantly. "You may think it's reckless or nutty, but I want to see if he'll stay with me if I take his lead rope off."

"You mean out here in the wild-blue?"

"Yes. So if he wants to leave me, he can, but I don't think he will."

Walter unclipped the rope from Zeus' halter and took several steps back, and said, "I know you could just take off, but I trust you. You know my heart, and I know yours. We're brothers."

The photo I captured of that moment was priceless.

They *boys* walked side-by-side down the path. No rope. No restriction. Only freedom.

Freedom between friends — between brothers.

Walter transformed the photo into a sketch. The detail was stunning. The veteran captured every nuance and created a masterpiece.

Walter caught the glimmer of affection in Zeus' eyes, the magnificence of this gelding's massive form, and yet, the gentleness his soft, rounded neck revealed.

This horse found his purpose, and this veteran rediscovered his passion.

This horse's heart was transformed by the love of a lost veteran. And this lost veteran's heart was transformed by the love of a horse, and the love of His Heavenly Father.

Father, thank You for loving us so much that one sincere confession and request for Your forgiveness is all it takes for You to bless us with Your amazing grace. Thank You for Your promise in 1 John 1:9 NIV—"If we confess our sins, He is faithful and just and will forgive us our sins and purify us from all unrighteousness." In Jesus' name we pray. Amen.

Author Note

God created horses as sentient beings. He created them to experience a wide range of feelings and emotions, from joy and contentment to anxiety and grief.

I'm so grateful for that.

Mr. Webster's definition of such a creature is so poignant.

"A sentient animal is one for whom feelings matter" (John Webster, Professor Emeritus, University of Bristol).

Horses recognize social relationships, the related behaviors, and discern between choice and consequence. They desire to quiet our hearts, soothe our hurts, and help us find hope.

This is why—year after year—we continue to choose horses to help us do our therapy work, and why we insist on keeping God at the center of our world.

God is flooded with our love when we choose to spend time with Him. Not to ask for a solution to this problem, or that challenge. Or to supply a miracle or avert a disaster. But rather, when we simply rest in His presence as a friend and follower.

God is overjoyed with us when we turn towards Him and match His pace. Whether it's back to the barn, down a new path, or anywhere He leads. I believe He smiles when we read about Him, talk to someone about Him, or sit quietly just waiting for Him.

God is pleased with us when we choose to grow our relationship with Him. When we trust it will always result in a treasured connection, a valued relationship, and the invitation to ride into eternity with Him.

End Notes:
- http://www.thehorses.com
- http://www.parelli.com
- http://www.equinehelper.com
- http://www.animalcognition.org
- https://dva.wi.gov Wisconsin Department of Veteran Affairs
- https://www.va.gov United States Veteran Affairs
- https://wicvso.org Wisconsin County Veteran Service Officers Organization
- https://eagala.com Equine Assisted Growth and Learning Association
- https://pathintl.com Professional Association of Therapeutic Riding International
- http://www.healthline.com
- http://www.maketheconnection.com
- http://www.mentalhealth.va.gov
- http://www.nctrc.org
- http://www.safehelpline.org
- Suicide Prevention Hotline: 988
- Sexual Assault Support Hotline: 877-995-5247
- *From the Horse's Point of View* by Debbie Steglic
- *Horses Speak* by Sharon Wilsie
- *The Equine Listenology* by Elaine Henry

ACKNOWLEDGMENTS

To the veterans who allowed their stories to be told, thank you. Because of your courage and selflessness, you will help change and save lives. Without you, *Unlikely Recruits* would not exist.

Special appreciation to my husband, William, a U.S. Air Force veteran, Trinity co-founder, and my biggest cheerleader. Thank you for always believing in me. I love you so much.

A million thank you's to my compassionate and talented teammates at Trinity Equestrian Center whom I've had the privilege of working side-by-side and learning from for so many years, especially my decade long therapy partner and dear friend, Sylvia Piekarz, and my sister Jan Behm, Trinity co-founder.

To my family whose love and encouragement helped create the space needed for me to finish this journey, I thank you. Love you, love you.

Cynthia Ruchti, my legendary agent who blessed me with your expertise and tireless patience, thank you for mentoring, encouraging, and loving me throughout this journey of shaping this book and its impact.

Gratitude to my sister Cathy Klick, who was often my sounding board throughout my writing process.

My dear friends who have shared their love, support, kind words, endorsements, and eagerness to become this book's raving fans, thank you, and I love you back.

My awe of God my Savior knows no limits. Thank You for urging me to write and accompanying me the entire way.